RANDOM ENCOUNTERS WITH THE SUPERNATURAL

by

Jane Horton

Jon,
You made an inspirational impression on my life that has led me to becoming a published author.
Thank you Cousin,
Jane Horton
2/17/23

DORRANCE
PUBLISHING CO
EST. 1920
PITTSBURGH, PENNSYLVANIA 15238

Dorrance Publishing Co
585 Alpha Drive
Pittsburgh, PA 15238
Visit our website at *www.dorrancebookstore.com*

ISBN: 978-1-6853-7272-9
eISBN: 978-1-6853-7811-0

Random Encounters with the Supernatural is dedicated to my husband, Paul, and our children for your patience and support during the many years I have been writing our family's supernatural stories. To my friend, Joanna, you listen, share, and inspire all who know you. Thank you for opening my eyes to a living God and Devil that supernaturally affect our lives in today's world.

The majority of the names of living and deceased people
have been changed to protect their families and personal privacy in
Random Encounters with the Supernatural

TABLE OF CONTENTS

Author's Mother and Grandfather

Entrance to the Camp Chesterfield

INTRODUCTION

My initial purpose in writing this book was to chronicle my family's supernatural experiences to pass down to my children. I originally thought there would probably be around ten or so stories of interest. Thus far there are close to seventy major experiences involving three generations.

I did not grow up in a household where the paranormal was a topic of conversation. Whatever label which best describes these manifestations infrequently occur when I least expect it. My mother had mentioned during the 1920s her father, mother, and a great aunt often attended a spiritualist camp in Chesterfield, Indiana. The camp was established in 1886 for the purpose of communication with deceased love ones through mediums. This was the extent of the information passed down to me.

My childhood was spent in rural Florida before Disney World changed the image of the state. In the 1960's, Florida was considered southern and traditional and not the melting pot it is today. People saw life in a straight forward manner based on conservative values.

My father was retired from the United States Air Force as a Lt. Colonel, a veteran of World War II and Korea. My mother, also a veteran of World War II, served as an Army Air Corps nurse. Both of my parents descended from pioneer stock, strong in character and values. They followed a moral code, no stricter than most practicing Christian families of the sixties. Mom and Dad were not rigid in their religious beliefs. My parents were raised to attend church on a mandatory basis. They resisted this routine in their adult years, explained by their disapproval of organized religion. They were open minded and the antithesis of superficial.

I didn't take my supernatural experiences too seriously for many years. By the time I was in elementary school, I realized not everyone had these experiences or believed in them. This is not a subject I would bring up for the sake of discussion for fear of being ridiculed by my peers. Mind you, most of my childhood friends were Southern Baptists. It would have been socially unthinkable to speak of my encounters.

When I was sixteen-years-old, my father died from lung cancer and an aortic dissection. I was deeply affected by his death. He continued to reach out to me beyond the grave. Dad visited me in my dreams. The smell of cigarette smoke was occasionally detected in our home and car. If we moved, the experiences continued in our new home. His comforting words of reassurance and guidance would pop into my head just when I needed his advice. This ignited my spiritual curiosity to question the fine line between these two planes of existence.

People are generally prone to reject what may not be easily explained. By nature we don't appreciate change and are skeptical of things we don't understand. I do believe it is wise to question the validity of our experiences and not to accept them at face value.

The Bible states in John 4:1, "Dear friends, do not believe every spirit, but test the spirits to see whether they are from God, because many false prophets have gone out into the world."

Jesus advised in Matthew 7:15, "Watch out for false prophets. They come to you in sheep's clothing, but inwardly they are ferocious wolves."

In 1 Thessalonians 5:20-21, "Do not treat prophecies with contempt, but test them all; hold on to what is good."

Jesus was the greatest healer and psychic the world has known. Two thousand years ago, a thirty-three-year-old carpenter performed miracles in the name of God. Men in positions of power, both religious and governmental, grew jealous of the impact this simple man had on the masses, so they crucified him. Christ rose from the dead and ascended into heaven. Christians accept this as fact because it is documented in the Bible, a book written by men assigned by God. So why do Christians and non-Christians jump at the chance to label those who witness supernatural events as being fraudulent? Self-proclaimed prophets claim they have dreams of wars, earthquakes, and disease. Christians accept their word as gospel, if the prophet proclaims the message came directly from God.

I have attempted countless times to deny and repress my past life memories, astral travel, premonitions, clairvoyance, clairsentience, and clairaudience experiences. I knew by being candid I would be socially rejected and considered a prime target of a Christian fundamentalist youth group to convert and save me from evil influences of the dark side. It was best to blend in and keep quiet. As a teenager, I belonged to several Christian youth organizations and held leadership roles. I have always believed in God and Jesus Christ as my savior. I wanted to be like everyone else my age, but I wasn't like everyone else.

By the time I was in high school, I felt more secure with myself. In one particular class in my junior year, I spoke candidly of my belief in reincarnation. My amiable relationship with my World History teacher quickly turned sour. By the look on his face, I knew it would be best not to say anything further. On my next report card, he gave me a C in conduct. Never before or since did I have a blemish on my conduct record.

Over the past ten years, I have met Christians that believe God still creates miracles. Those miracles are supernatural. I can no longer brush aside events in my life that are responsible for leading me down the path of spiritual understanding. We must have faith in God. I have come to accept that I cannot plan my future. Whenever I try to control my path, fate steps in and takes control. God has a plan for each of us. He will lead the way if we let him. We do have the ability to make choices. If we ask God, he will assist us in making the wisest decision.

The world has become more open minded to the supernatural,. It seemed to change with the publication of actress Shirley MacLaine's book, *Out on a Limb*. Today every evening seems to have a ghostly encounter show on television. If it were not for Miss MacLaine initially going out on that limb to pave the way for us to follow, the public would continue to reject the supernatural.

During the past thirty years, the media has reported so many firsthand accounts on television and in the press. The Travel Channel televises one paranormal episode after another. Why don't they just call it The Supernatural Channel? On a few Christian channels, host Sid Roth of *It's Supernatural* interviews people who have walked into the supernatural with God, Jesus, angels. deceased loved ones, and experienced demonic encounters. The majority of adults now believe in some form of the supernatural.

Modern technology has made affordable instruments readily available online to the general population that provide scientific proof validating there is more to our world than meets the eye. Digital cameras, high speed 35mm film, smart phone cameras, digital recorders, electromagnetic frequency detectors may be purchased for less than $100. You don't have to have a PhD. in Parapsychology to photograph orbs, ectoplasm, shadowy images, and record voices.

Every once in a while, I receive a reading from a medium. I refer to my occasional readings as my checkups.

A medium at the Houston Psychic fair inquired, "When are you going to finish writing your book?"

Another psychic in Savannah, Georgia inquired, "Why don't you finish writing your book?" When I attended a Renaissance Festival in Plantersville, Texas, I decided to have a reading just for fun. The reading lasted forty-five minutes. Typically you pay $20 for twenty minutes. I was drained by the end of our session.

Once again I was asked, "Why don't you finish the book?"

I replied, "I already have written several stories to pass down to my family."

"Yes, you have, but you have not finished the book to send to a publisher."

My pat answer, "I fear rejection and I'm lazy."

"You have nothing to lose."

The encouragement from mediums was not enough. I continued to ignore their advice. Until one night in December 2007, I was channel surfing. A young man was speaking about the power of prophecy. Why did I continue to listen? His demeanor caught my attention. He was calm. There was no ranting, raving, or crescendo in his voice. A peaceful feeling came over me. At one point, he requested listeners to inquire for a free prophecy. Nothing in life is free. There is usually a catch, but I don't have to get hooked. I sent an e-mail requesting my prophecy. Two or more weeks later, I received a package from the ministry. I thought, well, it looks like I received a lot of propaganda, so there it sat on the table with all the other junk mail. Two weeks later, I finally decided to sift through the mail clutter and open the package. It was not a written prophecy but a DVD.

Later in the evening, I took the time to listen. A man announced the name of the inquirer, and four mediums took turns giving a phrase of prophecy for that individual. The messages were often predictable.

"Drink more water. Watch your health. Real estate."

Okay, I was duped, but it was free. I fast forward to avoid the endless alphabetical surnames before mine. When my letter in the alphabet became close, I braced myself. Would they mention my health or instruct me to go to the doctor? Tell me to drink more water and other miscellaneous bull that anyone in the world could identify with these messages? My personal message was: "WRITE THE BOOK." I nearly fell off the bed. I had not heard that same advice given to the other gullible inquirers. I guess someone thinks my experiences are worthy to be committed to paper, not just for my family but maybe for other people to read.

The stories detail the strange events that have touched my family, but I could not begin to keep track of the number of fleeting moments we all have experienced. I am referring to the times when a touch or pat on the shoulder was felt or the quick, shadowy movements have been seen from the corner of an eye. We have witnessed at one time or another a translucent image of a deceased cat rolling on the bed or feeling the jump on the bed of that missed little fur baby. Footsteps and muffled voices may be heard in an upstairs bedroom or hall. While two of my children have slept, socks have been removed and blankets pulled down. My son has been awakened by his shirt being pulled from the back, lifting him partially off the bed. When he quickly rolled over and told the ghost to stop and let him sleep, in response the ghost stomped so hard, it caused the nightstand and lamp to vibrate. It is as if he wanted to play with my son, but respectfully he let my son sleep. Our family is not afraid, only annoyed. We roll over at night and go back to sleep.

For the most part, they don't mean us any harm. Life as we know it may end, but it evolves into another form of energy connected to the world we know. Our worlds just seem to blend together from time to time.

Fast forward to April 2020. The world for the most part is shutdown. Nothing like Covid-19 has happened since the Spanish Influenza of 1918. I have no doctor appointments and no events to attend. It is just the grocery store, pharmacy, and the post office on my list of things to do besides household chores. I can't think of a better time to finish my book. Interruptions are at a minimum. It has taken a pandemic to get me to the point of finishing the book that has been on my mind for over twenty years.

What I have lived through is recounted in my book as the truth. My goal is not to convince the reader but to tell my stories. If the reader is unable to digest and accept my experiences, that is their prerogative.

1
FIRST REMEMBRANCES

Before I started kindergarten, I was aware of events that seemed out of the ordinary. Dad was an USAF Lt. Colonel, and my mother, who had also been in the U.S. Army Air Corps, was a registered nurse. My parents were told they could not have children. I was quite a surprise to them after fifteen years of marriage. As an only child, born to middle aged parents, my life was different than other children. We lived on an island on Lake Monroe. Our neighbors were also retired military. I was an outgoing, friendly, precocious little girl who loved to talk with people.

Beginning at the age of three, from time to time, I would repeatedly ask my mother, "Let's go visit the people who live in the yellow house."

My mother said, "We don't know anyone who lives in a yellow house."

I persisted, "Oh, yes, we do."

Finally one day my mother said, "What do the people who live in the yellow house look like?

I gave a detailed description, "The woman is tall and has short brown hair. The woman wore shorts. The man is not as tall and is sort of big. He is bald on top with black hair on the sides and back of his head. He wore black pants and a white shirt. They have two big boys. The house is on a hill with lots of tall pine trees around it."

My mother seemed stunned. She replied, "Yes, we do know people who look like that and live in a yellow house. They live in upstate New York. We last saw them a few years before you were born." My dad was silent. My mother did not speak about this until I was much older.

It wasn't until many years later that I confessed to my mother there was more to my memory. While my future parents were outside sitting on the patio furniture visiting their friends, the two boys were playing basketball. I was with a young man in the pine trees overlooking the side of the yard where the driveway and carport were located. I have no memory of our appearance, only of our telepathic conversation. It is my belief I was looking at my mother and father as prospective parents from a bird's eye view.

This concept of peering down on someone was difficult for a child to comprehend. Couldn't my parents explain this to me? Children expect their parents to know everything about the world. How disappointing to discover that they don't know! Since my mother was clueless and then uncomfortable, it was best to drop the inquiry. You may be thinking, how does a pre-school age child remember such details? I am fifty at this writing. The memories are as clear to me now as they were all those years ago.

My mother and father stayed home with me until I entered kindergarten. Since my father retired from the military, he spent a great deal of the time raising me after my mother returned to work as a nurse at a nearby children's home. My relationship with my mother was strained.

I recall on one occasion saying to my mom, "My last mother was a lot nicer than you." That stopped the conversation. She abruptly sent me out of the kitchen.

Although my parents were strong disciplinarians, my father played an active role in teaching me life skills. They never spoke baby talk and drew it to my attention if I did. By the time I was ten, I knew how to fish, target shoot, prepare a meal, garden, mow, iron, and do laundry. Dad and I played cards, checkers, basketball, baseball, and swam in a nearby spring lake. If he was building something, I was nearby with a hammer in my hand. It was a lot of fun growing up in the country. Occasionally a mother and her children would move into the neighborhood. The missing father was stationed in Vietnam. They never stayed very long.

For the most part, my contact with children was limited to school. Before I started kindergarten, I instinctively was aware that certain topics should not be discussed, namely ghosts, dreams, and memories of another life. My parents did not speak of the supernatural. Exposure to the paranormal through the media was limited during the 1960s. The Twilight Zone was the only supernatural television show I am able to recall. No one I knew spoke of events that seemed out of the ordinary. Only during the Halloween season, an occasional ghost story would be read as a precursor to the annual Halloween festival and trick or treating.

Author at 3 years old

2
BEDTIME GUEST

My parents had a nightly ritual for preparing me for bed. After reading me a story and saying prayers, it was lights out. I don't recall how many times this image came to visit me. I saw a gray shadow in the form of a masculine figure standing at the foot of my bed, looking down at me. Facial features were not apparent. The image stood stationary, never moving except to disappear. The first few times this event occurred, I hid under my covers.

As time went on, I grew more tolerant and curious of this figure. I decided to be brave and find out what or who it was. It did not talk nor do I recall any telepathic messages. I did not feel there was any danger. As I stared at the shadow while lying in my bed, it eventually vaporized. By the age of seven, I never saw him again.

3
LOOK BOTH WAYS

During the summer vacation, when I was nine-years-old, I would knit for several hours a few days a week at a yarn shop. I couldn't get enough of knitting. It came very easy to me. One particular day, there was another girl learning to knit at the shop. We decided to get a drink at a convenience store across the street. She seemed to enjoy taking risks, so she suggested we run across the two lanes of traffic when the cars were quickly approaching. She made it across with a few seconds to spare. Perhaps she was experienced at this sort of thing. I, on the other hand, rarely took chances. She called for me to cross. It looked dangerous to me. I started to run and did not even look at the oncoming traffic. A firm, loud masculine voice in my head told me to stop. There I was on the double yellow line with a car in each lane passing me, simultaneously blowing their horns. When all was clear, I made it to the other side of the highway.

Upon entering the store, a clerk said, "You almost got run over! You sure are lucky." At the time, I was thinking there is no such thing as luck or coincidence. Someone was looking out for me. Afterward I remained leery of giving in to peer pressure.

4
BOYS WILL BE BOYS

When I was in the fifth grade, I had a dream of a young woman wearing a somewhat shiny, dark striped long dress standing at the bottom of a large spiral staircase. She had brunette hair pulled up and a fair complexion resembling me but older. She was pointing her finger at two dark haired boys close in age, approximately seven to ten. One of the boys had curly hair. They both wore overalls. She firmly admonished them as her finger repeatedly went up and down.

"Don't you ever play no dido on me!" I do not remember any more of the dream.

The next morning, my father said, "Boy, that was some dream you had last night."

"What do you mean?"

"You were giving someone the dickens."

"What did I say, Dad?"

"Don't you play no dido on me!"

"What is a dido?"

"It is a mischievous trick."

This dream and a future dream pertaining to another previous life reoccurred during my childhood. Today they are just as clear in my mind as they were over fifty years ago. The dream of being a mother of mischievous boys in the 19th Century has never left me. I pursued its origin into adulthood. The dream's details came many years later in a regression covered in Chapter 40.

5

THE BRIDGE

I had a recurring dream of a woman driving a dark old model car at night. Although I was only in elementary school at the time of the dreams, I knew the woman driving the car was an older version of me. I navigated along a dirt country road during a thunderstorm. My destination was home, where my children and husband waited for my arrival. The bridge ahead of me was the old architectural style with metal bracing over the road.

While crossing the bridge it was so dark, I could not see ahead. Suddenly I felt the car begin to plunge over the edge about midway across of the washed-out bridge. Each time I had this dream, I would always wake up just as the car began to descend. All I could see were the lights reflection on the black water but never the actual impact.

I have feared bridges most of my life. It has been a phobia that I have wrestled with, especially when I obtained my driver's license. If I was forced to drive over tall expansion bridges, I would hyperventilate.

When I was regressed over forty years later, the events responsible for my accident became known. The regression helped me to overcome my fear of bridges.

6

UNIDENTIFIED FLYING OBJECT, UFO

My father decided to retire from the Air Force during the late 1950s. We settled on a beautiful idyllic location called Stone Island on Lake Monroe in Florida. This area was basically undeveloped. A few retired military officers and professionals lived on this peaceful wooded habitat.

The closest town was Sanford about two miles across the lake. A naval base was located on the outskirts of town. Orlando also had Naval and Air Force bases. The Vietnam War was in progress at this time. Military air traffic frequently flew over the island; we were accustomed to the sight and sound of military aircraft.

My father and I walked most nights, weather permitting, enjoying the breeze and the stars. At this time, Central Florida was a beehive of UFO activity. We were open minded to the opportunity of a potential UFO sighting.

My dad was an early riser. He had a routine of turning on the radio, making a pot of coffee, reading the paper while sitting in the living room with a lakefront view.

While I was eating breakfast, my father mentioned to me he saw a saucer shaped object over the lake earlier in the morning. It had pulsating lights that surrounded the bottom circumference of the structure. He saw it silently suspended over the water, then take off, vanishing within seconds into the twilight sky. While reading the comics at the breakfast table, I listened to people speak of the UFO sighting on the radio.

"Dad, did you call in to report your sighting? They may believe you, since you were in the Air Force."

He did not report the sighting and made no further explanation. When I asked if he believed there was life on other planets, he said, "It would be foolish to think we are the only ones existing in our universe."

Dad showed me that in the first chapter of Ezekiel an UFO account is made by the prophet.

"As I looked, a storm wind came from the North, a huge cloud with flashing fire from the midst of which something gleamed like electrum. Within it were figures resembling four living creatures that looked like this: Their form was human, but each had four faces and four wings, and their legs went straight down, the soles of their feet were round. They sparkled with a gleam-like burnished bronze."

In Ezekiel 1:16, "The wheels had the sparkling appearance of chrysolite, and all four of them looked the same: They were constructed as though one wheel were within another wheel."

I do believe in UFOs, but I have not been given the opportunity to witness a sighting. The prevalence of digital and video cameras increases the likelihood of capturing their existence on film. Doubters insult eye witness accounts. You don't have to be a building contractor to recognize a structure's frame, plumbing, and wiring. Why do the naysayers think you have to be an astral physicist or pilot to clearly determine what is of this world and what is not? If the government has knowledge of flight vehicles that are as large as a football field and fly silently over our communities, the public has the right to be informed of their existence.

I often attended an UFO club while living in Houston, Texas. Each meeting began with an oral report for the month of the number of sightings in the State of Texas and in the United States. There were speakers and documentary films covering crop circles, aerial, underwater, and underground sightings witnessed all over the world. Attendees and guest speakers did not appear to be eccentric. The majority were professionals connected with the aerospace industry and law enforcement.

7

SHERIFF HOWARD

When you grow up in a rural community, you know everyone, or you know about them. I was not privy to the adult conversations of the house until this event occurred. My dad was friends with the local sheriff. I remember the sheriff was a man of medium height and stocky frame. His estranged wife was attractive and blond. They were always friendly to me.

As I recall, Sheriff Howard and his wife separated. She had a relationship with another man. The sheriff just could not take it anymore. One night he found them at a secluded local bar and threatened both with a gun. His wife and her lover ran for their truck. She was shot in the back. Her lover was shot in the face through the driver's window, both dying in their attempt to escape. Sheriff Howard drove home. He called our house. I answered the phone.

A strained male voice said, "Jane, this is Sheriff Howard. I need to speak with your dad."

I said, "He is asleep. I'll go get him."

Sheriff Howard replied, "No, don't wake him up."

"Okay. I will write down the message that you called."

The next morning, my dad had already left the house by the time I woke up. My mother recounted to me the tragic events of the previous night.

Here was a man that pledged to uphold the law. His life as he had known it was over. There was no way out of this mess, except to put a gun to his head and pull the trigger. Within one hour, three people were dead. The community was numb with grief.

Each year on the anniversary of the sheriff's death, our phone would ring at the precise time he called my father. There would be static and then the line would be dead.

We would say, "Oh, it must be Sheriff Howard calling." The phone calls stopped on the anniversary of his death in 1974, eight months after my dad died. I would like to believe this was a sign Dad and his friend the sheriff had met up in heaven.

8

DAD'S DEATH

My father died August 8th, 1973 at the age of fifty-four. Dad had been a heavy smoker. He died of lung cancer and a heart aneurysm. This was a month before my sixteenth birthday.

During the last year of his life, he drank heavily. We discovered after his death he had been aware that little time remained for him. Dad had underlined his symptoms and diagnosis in The Merck Manual medical book. My father didn't tell us, but as we reflected on his behavior and his actions, we surmised he was a man with little hope.

Within a month after Dad's death, on the same night, Mom and I dreamed of Dad walking down our driveway. In both of our dreams, he appeared to be solid. He was wearing his favorite clothes: khaki slacks and a plaid shirt. The dreams were personal to each of us. In my dream, the goodbye was between my dad and me. In my mother's dream, the goodbye was between Dad and her. I was standing on the front porch. He did not climb the stairs to the porch but stood at the ground level I had a feeling we should not touch.

I said, "Dad, you're back."

Dad replied, "I didn't get a chance to say goodbye." We told one another that we loved each other. He turned and walked down the driveway. When he reached the road, he stopped, waved, and then vanished as he began to walk. It was a touching ending to our last farewell.

9

DAD'S HERE

A year after my father passed away, we moved closer to my high school. One Sunday afternoon, I was studying in the living room. Mom was in the kitchen. The smell of Old Spice slowly filled the room.

I called, "Mom, could you come in here? Take a deep breath and tell me what you smell."

Mom stated, "It smells like your father's Old Spice."

Another time we had a thunderstorm with considerable lightning. After lightning struck a lamp in the living room, I smelled something burning. The smell was distinct. It was not an electrical smell but a burning cigarette. Once again my mom confirmed she smelled the same odor. It was comforting to know Dad was watching over us.

10

CASSADAGA

Prior to the information age, access to paranormal information was limited. Literature was scarce, only to be found at specialty shops that catered to the children of the Age of Aquarius, not mainstream America. We received reception from the three main television stations. Cable did not exist. I only remember programs about the Bermuda Triangle and Atlantis.

Since I was a child, I had been aware of a nearby town called Cassadaga, where the residents were mediums or psychics who talked with the dead. The Spiritualist camp has changed little in appearance from when it was established in 1876. It is off the beaten path, and at one time there was a gate preventing the curious from trespassing off the county road onto the narrow winding lanes where psychics' Victorian homes were nestled among the pines and live oaks dotted throughout the hills of this mystical Florida pioneer town.

Local people, for the most part, shied away from Cassadaga. A Roman Catholic friend of my mother's occasionally visited a medium, Reverend James Buchanan. He was an ordained Spiritualist Minister. He had an excellent reputation for accuracy as both a medium and a psychic. A medium communicates with the dead. A psychic is able to foretell future events.

At sixteen I decided to drive to Cassadaga with the hope I would receive a message from my father. I was apprehensive driving by myself and told no one of my purpose. Perhaps my own experiences would be validated. After I parked in front of his old wood framed home, I was taken off guard by the color of his house. The outside was painted black with white trim. Would he also be eccentric in his manner and dress? I was nervous, but when this jovial, blond, cherub faced man with a resonating voice greeted me at the door, I immediately relaxed. He asked me to have a seat and excused himself from the room. What was he doing behind the closed French doors? Perhaps he was clearing his mind. He did not know me or how I was referred to him. Don't give any personal information unless the medium wants validation they are on the right path of the reading.

He returned shortly and sat behind a small secretary's desk. He instructed me to have my feet flat on the floor. I was not to cross my legs or arms. He began our session with a short prayer to God. After the prayer, he immediately spoke of feeling chest pain. He physically appeared having difficulty in breathing. His voice was labored as he spoke of a father figure standing behind me. I confirmed my father was deceased. Reverend Buchanan communicated my father was sorry to leave and not say goodbye. He apologized for not always being the best father.

This was the beginning of ten years of what I called checkups with Reverend Buchanan. I attended psychic fairs and visited other medium/psychics, but none compared to Reverend Buchanan. I felt very connected to him. He suggested I study in Cassadaga to develop my gift. The idea was tempting, but I was focused on my own path as a young woman living in a traditional world. It wasn't until many years later I came full circle and took his suggestion.

11

CLAIRSENTIENCE EXPERIENCE

During the summer of 1976, I participated in a French study abroad program. The students were able to venture wherever they wanted to go without a chaperone for the last two weeks of our stay in Western Europe.

On one of our many stops, my friend Sherry and I decided to tour the small town of Dachau on the outskirts of München, Germany. Dachau was the location of a concentration camp for prisoners of war during World War II.

We stopped by an information counter located in the subway station to inquire about directions. The woman said, "You don't want to see that. Not much is there. It is very depressing." Sherry and I insisted we wanted to see where it had been located. It may have been a morbid spot to visit, but it was historical.

On that overcast rainy day, we took a subway as far as we could go, then transferred to a bus. We were dropped off at the gates of what was once the site where thousands of political prisoners dropped off the face of the earth. Several of the original buildings still existed in the camp. Almost all the barracks were gone, but there was a diagram depicting the layout of the camp. Countless pictures were on display. A monument of intertwined bodies resembling barb wire depicted a graphic and poignant representation of bodies wrenched in pain heaped on top of one another. On the day of our visit, a group of Orthodox Jews ceremoniously placed a wreath at the base of the monument.

The images will never leave me. I positioned myself outside centrally where the barracks of prisoners once stood and gradually pivoted 360 degrees trying to absorb from the landscape what feelings of despair were endured by the suffering of thousands of victims. As I walked around the camp, where only the outline of each barracks perimeter was marked, there was such stillness in the air. The ugly reality of the massacre of thousands of innocent people was foreboding. I was overcome with emotion attempting to hold back the tears.

My friend and I stepped in line with others to walk through the gas chamber that resembled a communal shower. Shower heads were in the ceiling. I felt sick to my stomach and was eager to vacate the building. Nausea and dizziness encapsulated me.

There was a sign in the communal shower stating it was never used as a gas chamber. In search of the truth, I read there is no evidence of gas chamber equipment having been installed and utilized at Dachau. You couldn't convince me it was only a shower. It had been thirty years since the end of WWII, and the smell of gas was still apparent to me.

I have reflected on this visit, surmising I was just sensitive to the odor. Why could some people smell the gas while others could not? Did I have a clairsentience experience or an active imagination? I believe it was the former.

12

CHURCH SERVICE

The service of a Spiritualist church is similar to a protestant church. Modern and traditional Christian and inspirational songs are sung. There is a prayer service and collection similar to Christian churches. Today the church does not focus entirely on Christianity, but other religions are acknowledged. The message given by the guest speaker is the big difference. The message is not only given by the speaker but by the spirits from the other side that come to join their loved ones.

One Sunday morning, my mother and I decided to attend The First Spiritualist Church of Cassadaga. On this occasion, the guest speaker was a woman named Eloise Page, a respected medium/psychic. She gave open mini readings to various members of the congregation at the end of her presentation. After a few readings, she looked directly at me. There was a large picture of Jesus suspended above the stage behind the podium. Almost immediately the picture of Jesus appeared to be right in front of me as if it zoomed into focus like a camcorder lens. All I could see was Eloise and Jesus emanating a bright white light. The light was so bright, I was striving to concentrate on what she was saying to me instead of feeling the intensity of the light. It wasn't a painful experience, although tears fell down my cheeks. I felt love and compassion through the touch of the Holy Spirit.

Eloise foretold within the year I would become critically ill, but I would recover. She saw my father above and behind me.

After the reading my mother said, "What was wrong with your eyes? You were squinting."

I described the sensation created by the light. My mother, a nurse, attempted to rationalize this experience. It may seem incredulous, but I had a supernatural experience with Jesus.

The next year, I transferred to the University of Florida. I started to feel lethargic early in the semester. Maybe walking around a large campus in the heat had made me feel so tired. A week before finals, my tonsils were so enlarged, they partially blocked off the back of my throat. No one knew the cause of my illness. I was considered critically ill and quarantined at West Volusia Hospital in DeLand. My physician ruled out diphtheria. After several tests came back negative, he personally ran a test. This time it was conclusive, mononucleosis. I recovered from the mono and had a tonsillectomy four months later. It was a long recovery. I was extremely weak. Eloise's prediction became true.

I made an appointment with Eloise a year later during my spring break from college. I confirmed her prediction of my illness. During this visit, she warned me I would meet a man who had financial problems. The relationship would be short-term and could become violent. Within the month, I entered into a relationship with a smooth talker that left my head spinning. This roller coaster ride of a relationship ended after five weeks. Thankfully I came to my senses and had the love and support of my mother to eradicate this man from my life.

Colby Memorial Temple, Cassadaga, Florida

Reverend Eloise Page Meditation Garden, Cassadaga

13

MY AURA

I came home from college one weekend during the summer of 1977. In the early evening, I happened to be in the living room sitting in a chair opposite a large decorative mirror. When I glanced up, I could see a rainbow of colors surround my head. The multi-color aura was distributed evenly about a foot or more above my head, extending from shoulder to shoulder. The walls of my mother's living room were beige in color. This neutral background enabled the colors to stand out. Since this time, I have seen many auras but not at a quick glance in the mirror, only by focusing on the individual.

14

SAVANNAH

While visiting a college friend who lived near Brunswick, Georgia, we decided to drive an hour north to see Savannah. We drove down to the riverfront. It had been overcast and sprinkling most of the day. I kept suppressing this feeling there was someone I knew who lived in Savannah.

Finally I blurted out, "You are going to think I'm crazy, but there is someone (male) in Savannah that I know from high school. It is as if I wanted to go through the phone book and look for him." My friend gave me a blank stare. I didn't say anything further.

One year later, I discovered who lived in Savannah. He would eventually become my husband.

15

PREMONITION

I began to work at Embry-Riddle Aeronautical University a year after my college graduation. Everything in my life seemed to be falling into place. I had my own apartment, new car, job, and friends.

One evening I was at a male friend's apartment watching a television mini-series called Shogun. All of a sudden, I blurted out, "Within a month, I am going to meet someone from my past that I am going to marry." I don't know why I blurted out this news bulletin. It just came to me. How does one respond to these statements? It was typical of my friends to look at me and say nothing.

Two months later, I was attending an orientation for new employees held in the Student Center. During a break, I was engaged in conversation with a woman when all of a sudden, I felt as if someone was nudging me on my shoulder. I tried to ignore the nudge, but it was very persistent. I jumped up and excused myself to the restroom. I'm wandering while walking down the corridor, why did I do that? I don't even have to go.

Upon opening the door to leave the restroom, I passed a tall bearded man. He called to me. "Jane."

I turned around, thinking the voice sounded familiar. He was tall with broad shoulders, a black beard, and shoulder length messy blondish hair.

As I walked up to him and looked into his eyes, I said his name, "Paul."

We had Spanish class together in tenth grade. Secretly I had a crush on him, but he went for a wilder type, the kind who wore hot pants. We spoke briefly, catching up on five years since our high school graduation. Paul had been stationed at Hunter Air Field, Savannah, Georgia. He was in Savannah when I was there visiting with my friend. I knew there was someone I had known that lived in Savannah! After being honorably discharged, he registered at the university. I needed to return to my orientation but invited him to stop by the Registrar's Office where I worked.

That was the beginning of our relationship. We were psychically connected. I would sense he was in the building. I got up from my desk on many occasions to look for him in the hall. There he would be walking towards my office. On one occasion, he called me from a phone down the hall. I told him it felt like he was in the building. He was impressed by my sixth sense. We have now been together for forty-one years.

16

ADVICE FROM THE GRAVE

Being young and in love is an exciting time. Paul and I were talking of marriage. I was convinced he would be the one, but I wanted confirmation. A visit to Cassadaga was on my agenda the next time mini readings were to be held. The medium was not much older than me. I purposely made no mention of my plans or details of my life.

She was accurate about my work and friends, but I was there to receive more insight into my relationship with Paul.

She began, "Your father says a marquise diamond engagement ring would be nice, but it is the thought behind the ring that counts."

I was stunned. It wasn't quite the insight I wanted, but it came from my dad. That is the kind of advice he would give me. It was comforting to know he was aware of what was going on in my life. When I received a round solitaire engagement ring at Christmas, I was thrilled.

17

CONDO GHOST

In the early 1980s, my mother moved into a townhouse complex. Each town home had a different style of architecture. The center of the square had a massive oak tree, and the grounds were landscaped. Each condo had firewalls between one another. It was a lovely setting. My mom was happy with her selection.

While my mother was visiting a friend out of state, I stayed at her home. One night I was awoken by the sound of a man moaning. I took a glass and placed the open end against the bedroom wall. The moaning sounded like it was within the wall. I had never heard any of the neighbors prior to this time, but my mother had spoken of a man's moaning voice. I had not taken her too seriously since she was a little hard of hearing. I went back to bed and covered my ears with a pillow, eventually I fell back to sleep.

When Mom returned from her trip, I recounted my experience of the late-night moaner. My boyfriend Paul and I heard the moaning one evening while watching TV in the living room on the first floor. The living room and bedroom shared the same wall.

On another occasion, I rapped on the wall with my knuckle hoping the moaning would stop, but it only grew louder. It didn't happen every night. Mom's next-door neighbor seemed to be in good health. He wasn't the friendliest man, so we did not mention the sound to him.

My mother and I attended a Psychic Fair in Cassadaga not long after the encounter. Mom did not mention the night time moaner to the

Reverend Buchanan. He commented during her reading she had a spirit that could be heard within a wall of her home. She confirmed this but said he did not seem to be a threat. The medium said the spirit had no business staying there. He advised her to demand that he leave. This was her home, and he was not welcomed. We knew a house was originally built on the property. The spirit was perhaps attached to the land.

The next time Mom heard the moaning, she spoke in a loud firm voice that he no longer lived there and he should leave her home. We never heard the moaning ever again.

18

DESIGNATED DRIVER

When my husband and I were newly married, we attended a festival called "Light up Orlando." My husband, brother-in-law, his date, and I walked the streets of downtown Orlando, Florida partaking of the food, music, and drink. It was in the fall when outdoor life is a welcome relief after the long hot days and nights of summer.

After midnight we decided to make the trek back home to New Smyrna Beach. My husband probably had the lowest alcohol content in his system, so he was voted the most likely candidate to drive us safely home. As he merged onto Interstate 4, the rest of us relaxed and drifted off to sleep.

It felt as though I had been asleep for a while when a kind male voice, called out to me, "Wake up!" I instantly awoke to find our car headed straight for the guard rail along the St. John's River Bridge.

I yelled, "Paul, wake up!" Without delay he instinctively turned the steering wheel to the left to avoid missing the guard rail. No one else heard the voice's warning. No one had trouble remaining alert for the remainder of the drive home. We counted our blessings and thanked our guardian angel for his warning.

19

TIM

After Paul and I married, we settled into our new life together. We bought our first home, and within a month, discovered we were expecting a baby. A few months later, Paul's childhood friend, Tim, moved in with us after accepting a job at Kennedy Space Center. Tim had recently graduated from a nearby university. Tim was outgoing and gregarious. We knew few people in the area. I was focusing on the new baby. It would be good for Paul to have his friend with us and to help share expenses.

Eleven months later, it was Friday the 13th. I had warned Tim to be extra careful that day.

Tim said, "Jane, you sound like you're superstitious."

I replied, "I sure am, so be careful." I didn't feel good about him taking his motorcycle to work, but he was a grown man. I wasn't his mother, only his roommate.

That evening I was home alone with the baby. Paul was working the night shift. I seldom slept well when alone. I knew Tim had attended a party with co-workers at a restaurant in Cocoa Beach. It was after eleven, and he had not arrived home.

It was close to midnight on that rainy evening. Headlights were shining through the den's window. What a shock to find it was a police car parked in the driveway. I walked to the door before he had a chance to ring the doorbell and wake up the baby. My first thought was Tim had been arrested for driving under the influence.

The police officer asked, "Does Timothy Kiley reside here?"

I replied, "Yes, he does, but he is not here right now."

The officer proceeded to give his account of Tim's accident. He was returning home on a less traveled road along the Indian River. Teenagers were known to park along a small stretch of this highway. A girl turned her car in front of him. He had little time to break as he slid under her car. The rear tires ran over his chest, resulting in massive internal injuries. It didn't look like he would survive.

During the next few hours, the hospital would call asking me to locate Paul. Tim was trying to hang onto life asking to see him. Paul was working at the launch pad at Kennedy Space Center. He didn't have a pager. He had always rejected wearing a pager. Security wouldn't answer their phone. Cell phones were not as prevalent in 1985 as they are today. I tried desperately to locate him, but by the time my message reached him, Tim had passed away.

I often reflect of the last few months of Tim's life. He was depressed about his relationship with his longtime girlfriend. He had asked her to marry him, but she said no. His father did not approve of his girlfriend. His father was a hard-core old cuss from Mississippi. Tim's company was transferring him to Vandenberg Air Force Base. This combination of factors would depress anyone.

Tim would sometimes say, "I'm going to ride my motorcycle into the bridge. I want to die."

My reply to Tim, "Don't say such things. The Devil will hear you."

He would just chuckle.

Tim had a lust for life. It totally took me by surprise to hear him say such words. I dismissed those comments due to his moodiness. There is no evidence he caused his fatal crash. I learned from this experience that words are powerful. Be careful not to speak of death, you may be decreeing a tragic outcome you had not sincerely planned on.

Strange things happened to Paul and me during the many months that followed Tim's death. The first evening without Tim, I was doing laundry in the garage. Paul was resting in the den. When I returned to the kitchen, he called for me to come into the room.

Paul stated, "Tim is here. The hairs on my arms are standing straight up. I feel tingly. I feel him standing beside my chair."

Neither of us saw anything, but as I extended my arm towards the chair, it felt tingly and cooler. This was not our imagination.

On the first work day after Tim's death, I was in the kitchen. Paul had gone to work early in the morning. I heard the front door shut a bit louder than normal. I always kept the front door locked. It definitely caught my attention. We didn't have a screen door. I went to investigate. No one was around. The door was locked as usual. Upon returning to the kitchen, I glanced at the clock. This was the time Tim would be leaving for work.

Cocoa, our calico cat, behaved strangely immediately after Tim's death. She slept on his bed, which she had never done before. The day of his funeral, we were backing out of our driveway, and Cocoa was walking towards the car. It was as if she wanted to give us a message. When Paul stopped to check for oncoming traffic, she leaped onto the hood, walked to the windshield, and began to make a loud crying sound. She had never behaved like this before or since.

Tim's father grew up during the Depression. One piece of advice Tim took from his father was never put your money in the bank. Tim mentioned to my husband, his brother, and me that his money was hidden in his room. After his death, we searched his bedroom but could not find the money. Within a few days after his death, I dreamed his money was in an envelope under the large braided area rug. I got out of bed and walked straight to his room. This time I moved the bed against the wall and found the envelop of money hidden in the middle of the area rug.

During the months following his death, Paul dreamed of Tim and him being together. In the first dream, Paul found Tim and himself sitting in a boat. The water was completely still and dark. They were surrounded by mountains resembling the Rockies. There was no vegetation in sight. The two looked around at one another and their surroundings. No communication was exchanged. In another dream, Paul would be riding in a convertible with Tim at the wheel. They shared a love for old cars. The two childhood friends had taken many a ride together.

It seemed like old times until Paul said, "This is great. It is like you never died."

Tim, exasperated, said, "Damn, you shouldn't have said that." The dream ended. As time went on, Paul learned not to mention his friend's death during their visits. It extended the length of their time together during each dream.

Several months later in another dream, Paul found himself riding in the convertible with Tim at the wheel. Tim held an envelope filled with money just like the one we had found under the rug.

As he threw the money down, he said, "Paul, when you die, this is all that people care about."

We were aware that Tim had made his brother beneficiary to his life insurance policy. He never anticipated his father would outlive him. Tim's father had been in frail health for years. His father and brother were at odds with one another over the insurance money.

One night Paul and I both dreamed about Tim. We found ourselves sitting with him in his grandmother's boathouse. This dream was far more surreal than the others. It appeared to both of us Tim did not have any eyes. His eye sockets were black. He seemed to be very depressed about his untimely death. We were uncomfortable with this visit from him.

The dreams have come infrequently during the two decades since Tim's death. The last dream Paul had about Tim was right before our thirty-year high school reunion. In this visit, Tim brought along another friend, Andy, who had died in a car accident a few years before. Paul found himself standing in a driveway talking to Tim and Andy.

They told him, "Since none of us are able to attend the reunion, we decided to pay you a visit."

Everyone dreams. Dreams are for the most part fragmented and confusing. If you can clearly remember the dream's details that stay with you for years to come, then the dreams are symbolic messages from the spirit world. Don't dismiss them. Remember them and cherish this special communication between our world and the other side.

20

NIGHT TERRORS

Paul and I were settled into our community after living there for five years. He enjoyed his job. I had worked but decided to be a full-time stay-at-home mom. I enjoyed being involved in charitable work. We had everything but the white picket fence. Our lives were going just as planned.

I began to have a reoccurring nightmare. It was brief but terrifying. Close your eyes and visualize in your mind being face to face with the scariest theatrical image of the Devil, Satan, Lucifer, however you may refer to him. His face would zoom into view as if we were almost nose to nose. Each time I had the night terror, I would wake up startled with fright. My husband recommended we say the Lord's Prayer to help me get back to sleep. The Lord's Prayer helped me to relax and feel secure knowing God was there to protect me. Unfortunately the night terror would return another night. No words were exchanged. His presence in my mind was confirmation he knew me and posed a potential threat to my soul.

21

OUT OF BODY

One night I dreamed I floated out of my body through the bedroom window above my head. While suspended in a large oak tree and gazing up at the stars, I thought how much fun it was to fly among the treetops. I haven't dreamed of floating above the trees since I was a kid. Suddenly I shot into the sky like a missile. I was surrounded by stars. I moved higher until I reached a point where there were no stars in sight, only a bright light surrounded by darkness. When I reached the light, there was a woman dressed in a white gown and white fabric covered her head. All I could see was this woman and the pure light enveloped us.

By this time, I was panicking that I had died in my sleep. I was thirty-one years old and not experiencing health problems. The woman and I did not openly speak with one another but communicated with our thoughts. I am thinking, there has been a mistake. It is not my time. I have a small daughter who needs me. I can't leave Amy. You have got to check. There must be a mistake.

There was what seemed to be a long pause. Her thoughts communicated to me, "It is not your time."

Just as I heard those words in my head, I felt a strong force pulling me back through this darkness, past the stars, and plummeting into my bed.

I sprung up repeatedly saying, "I'm home. I'm home."

My husband woke up and said, "You've always been home. You've been right here in bed."

47

I exclaimed, "No, I haven't!" and proceeded to tell him what I had just experienced.

Several months later, I realized I had not dreamed in quite a while about the Devil. It is my belief he knew my time was coming and wanted my soul. As God is a part of our lives, so is the Devil. He knows where to find us.

I felt elated after having my out of body experience. I might have been out of my body, but I was not out of my mind. Never have I doubted there was a God, but now I knew my name and address were in His book. I felt a part of him. I understood His love for us. Each of us has a mission to spend our time completing our task and thanking him for the opportunity to do so. We should live our lives praising him through the kindness and love we give to others.

22

VISITATIONS

When my daughter Rachel was four-years-old, she slept in a small bedroom next to the room of my oldest daughter, Amy. Rachel has always been a good sleeper. Her little girl praying night light made the white room glow. Bedtime began around 8:00 P.M. and wake up time was between 8:00 to 8:30 A.M. She seldom strayed from this biological time clock even into adulthood.

One night Rachel was awoken by a presence in her room. When she spoke of this encounter, she never said she heard a sound, only the feeling someone was in the room. When Rachel looked up, she saw my father standing in the doorway smiling down at her. She recognized her grandfather from photos. Dad was dressed in khaki slacks and a blue plaid shirt. She said he seemed to glow from the inside.

My dad said, "Hi there."

Rachel immediately covered her head with the sheet and blanket. She waited and then peeked out from the bedding to find he was gone.

Perhaps she was afraid to get out of the bed. I did not hear about Dad's visit until the next morning. After twenty-six years later, her story has never changed. I feel at peace knowing Dad is watching over us.

On another occasion, when Amy was around twelve, Paul and I had stepped out of the house to run errands. When we returned, Amy proceeded to recount an experience she had earlier while we were gone. Amy was in the upstairs hall leaving her room to work on the computer in our bedroom. As she opened the bedroom door, she saw standing at the foot of our bed my father dressed in a white gown with a belt wrapped around his waist.

Dad asked, "Hello. Where is your mother?" Amy was speechless. Seldom for a loss of words, Amy froze and Dad disappeared. This was the only time he had been seen dressed in white. Amy no longer recalls her grandfather's visit.

23

MOM

In July 1993, at the age of seventy-seven, my mother had quadruple bypass surgery. Once she was stabilized, I was able to see her in intensive care. I was amazed at how bright eyed and rested she looked.

We chatted briefly, then she said, "Jane, I am going to tell you something that I would not tell anyone else, but I know you will understand. During my surgery, I found myself floating up to the ceiling and from a corner of the operating room I watched the operation." My mother had been a nurse for over forty years. She was very acquainted with surgical procedures but not out of body experiences.

I asked her, "Was anyone with you? Did you hear any voices?"

"No. I was by myself," she replied.

I said, "I believe you, Mom. What you had was an out of body experience."

Three months later, she suffered another setback and discovered she had colon cancer. In October 1993, my mother had a tumor removed from her colon. The doctor said if the cancer did not return within five years, she would be cancer free. Mom underwent chemotherapy for nine months. At the time, I was pregnant with my third child. We joked about our nausea and fatigue. Although she was nauseas and weak, she was thrilled she did not lose her hair. In fact she looked great.

In December 1997, my mother discovered the cancer had returned, but this time it was in her liver. She could have bought more time with us and had chemotherapy again, but she decided at eighty-two years of age, she had lived a long life. Why prolong the pain? She wanted to die with dignity, quietly in her own home. We called Hospice to come and assist her through the remaining months. If you are not familiar with this organization, keep it in mind if ever the time comes that you or a loved one needs their support.

Through the winter and spring of 1998, Mom's appetite and energy returned due to the medication. Summer had arrived, each morning I wondered if it would be her last day. I spent the evenings and nights with her. When I was with my younger children, my oldest daughter would stay with her grandmother. The three of us became extremely close during those last few weeks. Whatever we wanted to say, we said it. Mom promised she would try to contact us, if she was able to, and let us know she was alright.

Since the school year had ended, also my responsibilities as a preschool director of our Catholic Church. It had been a few weeks since being at work, so I decided to go to the parish office to help celebrate our priest's fiftieth birthday. Father Liam had finished opening his presents when a volunteer came into the hall to tell me my daughter was on the phone.

When I picked up the phone in the dining area, I said, "Amy is something wrong?"

She insisted, "Mom, you have got to come to Nini's house. Nini is talking to her father and your father." I knew this was a sign they were coming to help her crossover. I assured Amy I would be right there. I arrived at my mother's house in a few short minutes, but her visitors had left. Mom was very lucid. She spoke calmly that her father and my father had come together to prepare her. I inquired if she knew when she would leave. She only knew it would be within four days but not what day and time.

The next morning after Hospice left, Mom was sitting up in bed. She had her breakfast and a shower. Amy was lying on the bed alongside her grandmother. Mom smiled as Amy combed her hair. I was sitting on the other side of her bedroom.

Smiling, Mom asked, "Who are all these people in my room?"

"Well, Mom, I see you and Amy. I don't see anyone else. Do you know who they are?" I inquired. Mom shrugged and said she didn't know who they were. We dropped the subject. Amy and I both had goose bumps.

52

The next day, Mom was growing progressively worse. She wanted to sit in the den and watch TV. She had a glazed look over her eyes. Together the Hospice nurse and social worker came by to check on her. As we were sitting in the den, Mom looked at me sitting across the coffee table from her. She commented on how uncomfortable she felt with her mother being there.

The social worker said, "Do you mean your daughter, Jane?"

Mom said, "No, my mother is standing behind Jane."

The hairs on my arms were standing straight up. The Hospice staff didn't seem as surprised as me. There was a knowing look on their faces indicating to me that they had experienced similar situations with other patients.

I called my husband at work. I told Paul it didn't look good and could he leave work and help me. I would try to find an aide to help us care for Mom on a full-time basis. That evening after dinner, Mom and Paul were watching the Sci-Fi channel. Mom had asked Paul why he enjoyed fantasy shows. They were discussing the pros and cons of this form of entertainment. Later Paul carried Mom to bed. I wanted to stay with her a bit longer as he returned to the den.

While sitting on the couch watching TV, he noticed two rectangular shadows staggered, each approximately three feet by six inches glide across the beige carpet of the den towards the kitchen in the direction of my mother's bedroom.

Paul, an engineer, explained to me, "There is no way these shadows could have been created due to the lighting that was present between the den and kitchen."

I had a feeling it would be best to stay up in case Mom needed me. Within forty-five minutes, Mom began to moan and groan as she called out to me. When Paul and I reached her bedside, she said she was going home. Mom never used that expression. We eased her pain and made her as comfortable as possible.

Paul spoke in a soft reassuring voice, "Mom, try to relax and let go. Everything will be okay."

She wanted me to call Roberta, an aide, who had been helping her for several months. The two of them had an agreement that when Mom past, she would be there for her. I don't think Mom wanted me to be alone. Roberta would get off work at 11:00 P.M. and she would drive directly to

Mom's home. Mom was talking about going home and seemed to be uncomfortable, even though I had given her pain medication. While waiting for Roberta, I lied down beside Mom and told her how much I would miss her. In a way, I envied Mom and wished I could go, too. She would have no more pain or troubles. Her work was done, no more challenges to face.

Mom said, "It is not your time."

After Roberta arrived, Paul went home to be with the kids for the night. Roberta called to me, "I think you better come to your mom's room." She had started to let go. While I witnessed her death, I couldn't help but compare it to the reverse of giving birth. Instead of breathing out and pushing downward, Mom was breathing in as her chest moved in an upward motion. With her last breath, her diaphragm rose and relaxed, then she was still. The neighbor's two dogs, a Great Dane and white Pomeranian, began to howl.

I left the room to call Paul. The aide remained to tend to Mom. Paul and the kids would soon be here. I was worried he would arrive too early. The doorbell rang, and there was Paul barefoot and out of breath.

I said, "What happened to you?"

He replied, "I locked the keys in the house. I ran across the golf course. You need to drive me back to get my keys and the kids."

I was glad there was a delay. I had also called Hospice to inform them of Mom's death and to send a representative. When I returned from picking up the kids, I thanked Roberta for being a good friend to Mom. We said our goodbyes as she closed the front door behind her. The dogs continued to howl.

It is difficult to explain death to children. At the time of Mom's death, Amy was twelve, Rachel was seven, and Jack was three. I don't believe in shielding them from the truth. I planned to explain her death in words they would understand. They knew she would not be with us any longer. Talking about death, then experiencing the loss of someone who had been a major part of their lives were two different things. Paul, Amy, Rachel, Jack and I surrounded Mom's bed. We held hands and said the Twenty-Third Psalm. Little Paul repeated the words as best as he could. I explained her soul had gone to heaven. She was with her parents and their grandpa. We should be happy for her that she was no longer in pain. Death does not mean it is the end, but life continues in another place. They each touched her hair and left the room.

We waited in the great room for the arrival of the Hospice administrator and funeral home representatives. I was surprised to see the Hospice administrator was the same woman who called me the night Tim died. I remembered her name and voice. Although I did not know her personally, I knew we lived in the same subdivision. It had been thirteen years since Tim's departure. In a small town, we touch one another's lives in unpredictable ways. Once again another person we loved and cared for was gone. I thanked her for her kindness and the support of Hospice.

When Mom's body and Hospice had left, the dogs stopped howling. It had been over an hour of constant howling, each dog alternating. Paul, the kids and I returned home. It was the first time in three months I had slept in my own bed. How strange it seemed. As I lied in bed, I thought I'm a forty-year-old orphan. My mother was my confidant, friend, and my strength. We had our moments, but Mom played a big part in our lives. She helped me pull it altogether.

The next night after Mom's passing, my daughter Amy and I were sitting in the den of my mother's home. We were across the room from one another, reminiscing about Mom. I looked up at Amy and saw the outline of two figures, one taller than the other. Each figure appeared as multicolored sparkling lights. The figures had a pronounced glow of white light around the edge. I could not see facial features or clothing.

I commented to Amy, "We are not alone."

Amy exclaimed, "Don't freak me out, Mom."

"Don't worry. I think it is wonderful that they are here with us."

The figures then appeared behind me. Amy was amazed and frightened, my reassurances fell on her deaf ears. As soon as she acknowledged the figures, they vanished.

Mom kept her promise of letting us know she was with us. Within a few months of Mom's death, I was washing the dinner dishes. I felt a firm pat on my right shoulder. I spun around, but no one was visibly in the room.

One morning Amy was preparing to leave the house to catch the bus for school.

I called out to her from the family room, "I love you. Have a great day."

"I love you too, Mom," she replied as she closed the front door.

I felt someone pat the top my head. I looked around, but no one else was up. It felt like Mom's touch. I was comforted in knowing she was still with me, so much so I went back to sleep.

My daughter Rachel and I decided to visit my mother's grave. The cemetery was an hour from our home. We decided to make the day of it, just the two of us. We walked to the large Veteran monument in the middle of my parents' section of the cemetery. When we returned to Mom's grave, Rachel and I could hear the crush of grass blades behind us. Simultaneously we turned our heads to see who was walking with us. There was no one to be seen. That was the last time the two of us went to visit the cemetery together.

24

LEND A HAND

One weekend Paul was completing some action items on his honey do list. He was standing at the top of the stairs, and without thinking, tossed a screwdriver to Amy standing four or five steps below. She started to fall backward. I was screaming as I watched my daughter start to fall backward down the stairs, then she moved forward. Her knees were not bent. She did not grab onto the railing. Her body moved forward until she was standing firmly on the step.

Once I composed myself and gave her a tight hug, I said, "How did you do that?"

"I felt large hands push me back up the stairs." We were so grateful that someone was watching over her. My husband never again tossed a tool to someone standing on the stairs.

25

CHRISTMAS TREE ADMIRER

The first Christmas without Mom was difficult. She loved that time of year. We decorated the tree in the living room that was placed in front of a large picture window. I think people who passed by our house enjoyed the decorations as much as we did. After finishing the tree, I thought, well, now is the time I would call Mom to come over and take a look at our decorations.

When we sat down for dinner, I said, "Rachel, why don't you go turn on the Christmas tree lights?"

A minute later, Rachel said, "Mom, I think you better come in here."

All of us went to see what was wrong. The scent of my mom filled the living room. The lights on the tree glowed brighter, and a fist size ball of light zoomed from the tree between us and collided into the crystal chandelier in the entrance. The chandelier brightly glowed. My husband looked at me wide eyed with his mouth hanging open. We stood for a few seconds in total amazement of what we just witnessed.

I said, "I guess Mom wants us to know she saw the Christmas tree."

Mom returned each evening. The scent was not potpourri or a plug in. It was definitely Mom. It made us all feel uncomfortable. No one wanted to sit in the living room at night and look at the lights and decorations.

During this same holiday season, I was sitting in a wingback chair next to the Christmas tree while talking to a friend on the phone. I watched as a Christmas glass ball ornament went down and then up. It looked like someone was pulling it, then another ornament bobbed. I must be getting use to these odd occurrences because I continued with my phone conversation while watching different ornaments move. Mom must have grown tired of this game and stopped pulling on individual balls because I didn't acknowledge her until after I ended my phone call.

Christmas in our home buzzed with activity, and this Christmas was no exception, especially after the recent death of my mother. My husband Paul and I went shopping without the children. When we arrived home, our children and a friend of Amy's were outside on the sidewalk. They appeared to be waiting for us to return home. Amy recounted they were playing in the family room and began to notice a pungent odor meandering through the room into the entryway and living room. The children were panicking that the source could be an electrical outlet shortage or a gas line leak. When we entered our home, there was no trace of the smell. I became concerned that my mom's afterlife visits may have attracted a negative entity through a portal. It was time to sage and mist with Holy Water before the arrival of Christmas Day.

We gathered in the living room, opening presents while enjoying our new puppy dance around the paper and bows. The room started to have a fragrant smell of roses. The scent permeated through the living room to the entrance and then up the stairs. I was following the fragrance as it seemed to stop at the landing of the stairs.

"Merry Christmas, Mom. We love you. Mom, you need to go on and not be so tied to us." The aroma of roses verified to me that she was with God. After the scent vanished, we went on with the holiday celebration.

26

SOMEONE IS HERE

When Amy was a freshman in high school, she was a member of the Odyssey of the Mind team. This group of motivated teenagers worked together for many months following specific guidelines to problem solve in a creative format. When the product was completed, they would present it in a district competition. Four of the girls, including Amy, left home to spend the night at a hotel near the community college where the event was to be held the next day.

Soon after they bedded down for the night, strange occurrences began to happen. The air conditioner began to cling and clang in a rhythmic fashion. There was no earlier malfunction. Then the telephone began to ring with a soft tinkle of its bell. When one of the girls picked up the receiver, there was a static sound. The phone repeatedly made this noise, so one of the girls unplugged the phone. Each of these power glitches would not be considered paranormal, but the summation makes one question the source.

A few minutes later, my daughter saw the outline of a woman's body standing by the bedside of one of the girls. The image resembled a pulsating glowing light.

Amy said, "Someone's here. We are not alone." Of course they did not believe her, yet they would not open their eyes or uncover their faces to see the apparition. The uninvited guest disappeared. One of the girls divulged she had an aunt who passed away within the last week. Perhaps this would explain the apparition's presence near her side of the bed.

The girls chimed in unison, "She sees dead people." The giggling subsided; nothing further was said. After the incident, no one ever doubted Amy's truthfulness.

27

GOD'S GPS

In December of 1997, a friend of mine was chairman of her church Christmas craft show in Melbourne, Florida. My friend Beth and I, along with our daughters, decided to support our friend. We shopped and sampled the Christmas goodies, then decided to go to garage sales. We were driving in a fairly new neighborhood of contemporary two-story stucco homes. As we meandered through the subdivision reading directions from the garage sale signs, Beth drove to the left of a moving van as people were unloading their furniture.

My daughter, Amy exclaimed, "There's Sue, Ryan, and Charlotte!"

I said, "Beth, what town are we in?" My friend knew this town far better than I.

Beth responded, "We are in Melbourne, Jane."

I knew my longtime friend Sue returned to Rockledge and was living in a rental after her husband's job brought them back from California. Our lives were busy with work, family, and the children's activities. We lived in different towns and had not been keeping in close contact as we had prior to her move to California. Sue could be private about upcoming transfers and promotions in her life. If major changes were to be spoken to others outside the family, the potential change would somehow be jinxed.

Our friendship began some fifteen years earlier, when we both were newlyweds working in the same office at Embry-Riddle. Our husbands attended the university after leaving the military. We are godmothers to one another's second children. I asked my friend Beth to circle around and drive back by the house. I hesitated to stop, thinking Sue may be uncomfortable not calling to tell me she had moved.

Beth said, "This is too coincidental. Someone up there wants to bring you two back together. We are going to stop."

When we pulled up into the driveway, Sue's husband and son stopped unloading. They were glad to see us, and we laughed while giving each other hugs.

As Sue came out of the house, I said, "So you thought you could move and I wouldn't find you."

We squeezed one another and laughed so hard. Sue exclaimed, "An angel brought you here!"

We had always joked we must have known one another in a previous life. We can disclose confidences without the fear of judgment and criticism. Sue and I vowed to remain in contact for the rest of our lives.

28

TIMING

Zellwood, a small town in central Florida, sponsored an annual corn festival. Thousands from the surrounding counties made this annual pilgrimage to enjoy country music, crafts, rides, games, beer, and all the corn you would want to eat.

We usually attend the event with another family. This particular year, we caravanned with our friends Beth and Allen. Before we left home, we stopped by the Mobil gas station to fill our tanks and then it was onward to Zellwood. When we stopped at a stop light at the outskirts of Sanford, our friends pulled up parallel to our van. While filling the gas tank, their son's shoes were placed on the bumper and never retrieved before driving off. Since their little one was shoeless, we would need to stop by the local Wal-Mart to purchase another pair. This did delay our road trip, but oh well; there was no other alternative.

Thirty minutes later, we were back on the road and reached the west side of Sanford to discover twenty or so cars backed up along the highway. There was a police car and an ambulance assisting in an accident involving a car and a motorcycle. There were other motorcycles parked with their owners standing nearby. We were at a standstill. It was a beautiful spring day. As each minute went by, the line of vehicles grew longer. We waited another forty-five minutes before a medical helicopter arrived and air lifted the injured. This was time well spent counting our blessings for the detour to Wal-Mart and praying for those injured in the accident.

Forgetfulness is not a trait I would use to describe our friends. It was very probable that we might have witnessed this accident, or, worse yet, we may have been involved in the collision. It only takes a second to make the difference between life and death. Timing is everything.

29

GINGERBREAD VILLAGE

My children and I had planned to construct a gingerbread village while they were home on winter vacation in 1999. My oldest daughter, Amy, took the lead in planning the buildings and roads. Rachel enjoyed assembling the homes and spreading the white icing to cement the pieces together. We kept our eyes on Jack. He would sneak a piece of candy whenever he thought we weren't looking.

Once the village was created, I took a snapshot of their creation and placed the Polaroid on the kitchen counter to finish developing. They quickly sprung from the table while I was left to clean up. When all was quiet and the kitchen was back in order, I picked up the photo. I could see an arch of swirling light with small, round illuminated balls covering the children. The next morning, I took another photo of the children to see if the camera was defective. The next photo was void of anything unusual.

I attended a "ghost hunter" workshop in Cassadaga, Florida a year and a half later. I brought the photo with me to have an experienced "ghost hunter" examine the photo. He confirmed what I knew all along. This was energy enveloping the children. He referred to the light as a "hug from above."

Spiritual Hug

30

UNWANTED GUEST

My oldest daughter, Amy, planned a New Year's Eve party to celebrate the new millennium with her friends. We purchased fireworks from South Carolina, decorated the large screened porch in white with gold metallic ribbon suspended from one corner of the room to the other. Gold and white balloons were attached to the chairs and tables. Candlelight gave the room a welcoming glow of light. It wouldn't be long now until her guests arrived.

I was walking through the entrance headed toward the kitchen when I smelled an unpleasant odor coming from the living room. When I walked into the room, the odor grew more pungent, snigging my nostril hairs. If a spirit wanted my attention, they were successful. Fortunately only a few friends had arrived, and they were on the porch. I motioned to Amy to come into the house. I wanted her to substantiate the smell. Could this be a demonic entity or negative spirit?

Upon Amy's validation of the presence of our unwanted guest, I went to the china cabinet to get a bottle of Holy Water. We are Roman Catholic, so it isn't unusual for a Catholic family to have a bottle on hand.

I sprinkled the Holy Water throughout the house repeating with each hand motion, "In the name of the Father, Son, and the Holy Ghost, spirit be gone." Don't ask me how I knew what to say, it just came out of my mouth. As soon as I began the ritual, the foul odor vanished.

I never allowed Ouija boards in our home. The last thing I would want was to open a portal. We were having a lot of supernatural activity since the death of my mother. My family didn't need to have any additional activity causing them to worry.

I scolded the entity for trying to ruin Amy's party and that it was not welcomed in our home. The party was a success. There were no more signs of further activity for a while.

31

NINI'S FACE

One evening Amy, Rachel and I were in the family room watching TV. The room was illuminated by lighting along the perimeter near the ceiling. Amy sat in the corner of an L-shaped sofa. She saw out of the corner of her left eye something that moved through the doorway leading to the foyer. She quickly turned her head to see the translucent upper torso of her deceased grandmother.

My children affectionately called her Nini. According to Amy, her grandmother was expressionless but looked as she did prior to her illness. Amy quickly shut her eyes, stunned by this apparition, then opened to see Nini had vanished. Unfortunately Rachel and I did not see her. We were seated on another part of the sectional sofa unable to see around the doorway.

It is not abnormal to see movement in the corner of our eye, no matter who in the family is on the alert. Twenty years later, this is the only time my mother has visibly appeared to a member of the family.

32

FOOTSTEPS

During the winter vacation of 2000, Amy, Rachel and I stayed up late one night watching a movie on television. My husband and son had been to bed for many hours. Suddenly we heard footsteps coming down the stairs.

The sound of these footsteps was so loud, I'm surprised it didn't wake them up from a deep sleep. My husband and I had recently pulled up the carpeting on the stairs to refinish the oak flooring. Perhaps my son Jack was walking down the stairs, stomping down on each oak step. As soon as I rose from the sofa, the sound stopped. I walked to the foyer to turn on the light and continued to walk up the stairs, expecting to see Jack. To my astonishment, no one was there. The only sound I could hear was my husband's snoring.

The door to the air handler began banging. I quickly stepped back into the family room where the air handler was located on a common wall with the staircase. Our cat, Smokey, was wide eyed and rapidly pawing the door, causing it to bang, then he stopped and gazed up to the ceiling. We did not see anything out of the ordinary. Whatever Smokey saw must have disappeared because he looked at us and joined my daughters on the sofa. The hair stood up on the back of all our necks, including Smokey's furry back. We continued to watch the remainder of our movie. Everything appeared normal, and there was no point in ruining a good movie, although I don't know which was more suspenseful, the movie or the heavy-footed ghost.

33

CHURCH VISITORS

I was a preschool director at my church for four years. My oldest daughter, Amy, often assisted me with preschool productions. The end of the year play was "Noah's Ark." Amy was going to paint a backdrop of a large ark with an opening for the door in order for the children to exit the ark. We taped a large canvas to a wall in the church's multi-purpose room. This was a large room with a kitchen and a stage. After I helped Amy set up for what was planned to be several hours of work, I left her alone. There was no one present to distract her. I set the security system to give her additional safety. I left to attend to my other children and their after-school activities.

When I returned to the hall, she was packed up and waiting for me by the door. Amy had made excellent use of her time. The play's backdrop was taking shape.

Amy said, "Mom, I'm glad you are back, something strange happened while you were gone."

"What happened?"

"While I was painting, I heard a kitchen cabinet door begin to creak. I turned around and saw the door open almost completely by itself. The cabinet door then slowly closed."

"Why didn't you call me?"

"Nothing else happened. I'm used to things happening at home."

I thought maybe air coming out of a vent may have moved the door. It wasn't hot enough to have the air conditioning on. If it had been on, how could it have opened the door?

"You have gotten a lot of work accomplished, so let's load your supplies and go home."

On the evening before the play, we were at the main church hall setting up for the next day's rehearsal and evening performance. Amy and I had gone into the church to look for supplies in the Environment Room located in the main church adjacent to the hall. The church was dimly lit but visibly easy to walk through without turning on more lights. As we began to walk through the sanctuary, Amy paused.

She excitedly whispered, "Mom, I see a spirit praying." Once we walked outside of the church, she described a transparent figure kneeling in front of the first pew. She couldn't tell what gender, but it was dressed in a long robe. The spirit's head was bent down as if in prayer. I, on the other hand, did not witness this apparition.

While we were talking in the breezeway, which connected the church and hall, the smell of cigarette smoke became noticeable. Amy and I both smelled the smoke. We were the only ones at the church. We did not see anyone outside of the house up the hill from the church.

I said, "There have been enough strange things happening to us. Let's get out of here."

34

JUST PASSING THROUGH

One afternoon, not long before the children came home from school, I was walking through the family room. Out of the corner of my eye, the sight of khaki pants and a plaid shirt swooshed from the front door to the living room. I thought, that is odd, I didn't know Paul was already home from work. Occasionally, when I did not expect him home so early, he would sneak behind a door or wall and scare me as I walked past him. I crept into the living room and peaked around the wall, thinking he was about to spring out and grab me, but no one was there. I was home alone.

I believe it was my father paying me a visit. He wore his favorite style of clothes. The image did not appear solid due to its movement to a corner of the living room. I had visited a psychic a few months prior who stated my dad had been to my home and he liked the different front door wreaths I seasonally changed. It was comforting to know Dad popped in to check on me.

35

JACK

Our son, Jack, was an active tow-haired, blue-eyed little boy. At three years of age, I suspected he may have ADHD (attention deficit hyperactive disorder). Never before had I experienced a child who just could not sit down and listen to a story being read to him. He was a wiz at puzzles or video games. He stuttered and spoke in fragmented sentences, which added to his frustration in communicating with others. He had no fear of potentially dangerous situations. He was extremely impulsive, therefore increasing the risk of harming himself and possibly others.

With the love and patience from our family and his preschool teachers, he had made great strides in listening and getting along with others. He loved his preschool. At the age of four, Jack was planning to attend a field trip to the zoo. It was spring, and he had been suffering from hay fever, so I made an appointment with the pediatrician. I wanted him to be feeling up to par for this big day. The pediatrician prescribed an antihistamine and antibiotic for an ear and sinus infection. The next day, he attended the field trip. Upon his return, he was so happy and excited to have seen the dinosaur exhibit and ride the train throughout the park.

Early Friday morning, Jack began to vomit every two hours. He had a fever of 101 degrees. It was typical of our family to experience the flu during the months of February or March. We were concerned but not alarmed. After six hours, we were able to give Jack suppositories for his fever and encourage him to drink fluids to prevent dehydration. By Saturday he seemed to be improving, although he remained weak. He only got out of bed to go to the bathroom. As Jack lied in bed, he chuckled as he listened to the banter between his two sisters. The girls were never at a loss of derogatory comments to one another.

It was Rachel's eighth birthday on Saturday. Rachel was having a birthday party at the local bowling alley. We had hoped Jack would be back to his old self by this time. His fever never broke but fluctuated between 100 and 101. He was eating chicken noodle soup and drinking plenty of water, but on this day, he was very quiet. We left Amy at home to look after Jack for the few hours we supervised Rachel's party. Jack remained the same during Amy's watchful eye. Paul and I were hopeful the fever would finally break and he would be himself, bouncing around the house creating havoc as usual. Throughout the evening, Jack remained the same. Paul and I kept an eye on him throughout the night while we slept all together in our king-size bed.

The next morning, Jack was unable to get out of bed and walk to the bathroom. He complained of his head hurting. We didn't waste any time at this point. We were fearful he may have meningitis. We called the hospital to avoid delays in the waiting room and drove him to the emergency room. After examining Jack, the physician on staff ordered a spinal tap. Our little boy barely grimaced as the technician inserted the needle. We joked with one another to ease the tension of the situation while waiting for the lab results. When the physician returned, we learned Jack had traces of blood in his spinal fluid, but it wasn't conclusive he had spinal meningitis. He was admitted, and our pediatrician, Dr. Alden, was called. By this time, Jack was losing muscle control and his eyes could not focus but appeared to be wandering. He was prepped for an IV, an oxygen tube inserted in his nose, and the worse degradation of all, he had to wear a diaper. Dr. Alden was at a loss to the cause of his condition. He consulted other physicians, both on staff and through the internet, which lead him to the medical library. None of his research confirmed what our son was fighting. He decided it would be best to transfer Jack to Arnold Palmer Children's Hospital in Orlando, Florida. Our small-town hospital was not equipped to handle emergencies of this nature.

The nurses were compassionate, yet their eyes told me that his condition was becoming graver by the hour. Somehow I knew in my heart he would be alright. I called our priest, Father Liam, and let him know the severity of our son's condition. When Father Liam arrived, Jack did acknowledge him with a smile and a nod. I had not seen him smile all day until the priest's visit. Father Liam was known for his outgoing personality and fondness for the children. The children of our parish naturally reached out to him. As our parish priest extended his arm and gave a blessing, call it what you will, wishful thinking, blind faith, I had no doubt Jack would get through this. Paul did not share these feelings with me. Three hours later, a med EVAC team from Arnold Palmer arrived to examine and transport him to Orlando.

At first he was assigned to be isolated on the pediatric intensive care floor. Although no other family member had become ill, they wanted to rule out bacterial meningitis. A CAT (computerized axial tomography) scan was performed at 2:30 A.M. Monday. Hopefully it would indicate the presence of an infection in one or more organs. The doctors remained at a loss of what was responsible for his declining condition.

The doctor said, "Hold on for the ride. It will get worse before it gets better. He could possibly become paralyzed, blind, deaf, handicapped, or the worst, death."

The doctors prescribed a battery of antibiotics to be given with no clue which one would work. Paul stayed by his bed side. As much as I wanted to remain with them, the girls and I went home. We had no idea how long our lives would be out of the normal daily routine. I arranged for someone to care for our animals and keep an eye on our home.

Rachel and Jack's elementary school was very supportive and sympathetic. Many teachers and staff members called to say they placed Jack on their prayer chain.

On Monday morning, he had an MRI (magnetic resonance imagery). The neurologist ordered a brain activity test at 10:00 A.M. The test indicated no response. He was in a coma and possibly deaf. He had evidence of a severe sinus infection, which crossed over the membrane into his brain controlling his voluntary muscles. A diagnosis was still not conclusive, but it appeared to be viral meningitis and herpes encephalitis. The news was discouraging.

Paul's face showed the strain of the past few days. Paul rested at the Hubbard House, a lovely Victorian-style home for the families of patients. The girls and I stayed with Jack. Amy and Rachel quietly did their homework. Occasionally one of us would speak to him. He sat propped up with pillows in an upright position. His Teletubbie, Po, was at his side, and a Toucan beanie baby was perched on his pillow. He lied in bed, motionless and silent. His arms and legs began to stiffen and curl close to his body as he began to be in a fetal position due to the atrophy of the muscles. Paul began to massage Jack's rigid limbs. At this point, we felt we had reached rock bottom.

The severity of the situation was starting to take its toll. Paul accused me of not caring enough because I remained calm and unemotional. When a family faces a catastrophe, each member reacts differently. I cried and privately prayed. I was continuing part of my everyday responsibilities of paying bills, making sure our other children weren't losing hope, staying focused on their studies, and keeping family and close friends abreast of Jack's condition. I never lost faith that he would pull through this illness.

I called my friend, Beth, to bring her up to date on Jack's condition. She knew what we were going through.

I said, "Beth, it would do Paul a lot of good if Allen (Beth's husband) and Jerry (a friend) could come to the hospital and visit Paul. He is holding a vigil by Jack's bedside. He rarely leaves the hospital room." On Tuesday night, Allen and Jerry came to the hospital. They took Paul out for dinner listening intently as he vented his frustrations and fears. Afterward Allen took Rachel home to be with his family. They would see to it she went to school and got back to a normal life.

We alternated in shifts to be with Jack around the clock. During the late-night shift, Paul was alone with him. He sat in a chair next to the bed saying the rosary while counting the beads in his hands, asking God to give him a sign that Jack would recover. Paul said countless Hail Mary and Our Father prayers as he touched each bead of the rosary. While saying his prayers the morning of the third day, the rosary beads broke and scattered across the floor. As if on cue, Jack rolled his head towards Paul.

He looked directly at his father and said, "Hi, DAD," then smiled and rolled back into his coma. Did Paul really see what he thought he saw? For the time being, he told no one but me. God granted Paul exactly what he asked for, an indication that Jack would recover. I can't think of a better sign than waking up out of a coma and saying hello, even if it only lasted a few seconds.

Physical therapists started working with Jack on Wednesday. After his therapy, Paul and I stayed with Jack. I began to whisper in his ear,

"Jack, if you can hear me, move your ET finger." The device on his finger had a red light on it to measure the "oxygen saturation" in Jack's blood. He began ever so slightly to move his index finger of his left hand. I asked Jack to repeat it this time for Paul to witness the miracle. A male nurse came into the room to check on Jack. We told him what had just occurred, but you could tell he didn't believe us. This time I asked in a normal tone for Jack to once again move his ET finger, so the others in the room could also witness Jack's movement. The nurse was surprised as well. He asked Jack what was the name of his Teletubbie.

Jack said, "Po." Other nurses were called to witness the miracle.

In the early evening, the doctors were making their rounds. The nurses told the doctors that Jack was making one-word responses. The doctor made several attempts to converse with Jack, but he did not answer.

The doctor said, "It must have been a fluke."

A pretty woman physician in the group said, "Let me try to talk with him. Jack, what is the name of your Teletubbie?"

Jack simply responded, "Po."

Everyone chuckled, and someone commented, "Well, I guess he likes pretty girl doctors." Paul explained Jack's lack of reaction to the older male doctor could probably be due to the poking and prodding he received when the doctor came to examine Jack. A little boy doesn't understand why someone would do such a thing.

The next day, I walked into Jack's room to find him awake, sitting up in his bed.

With a big broad smile on his face, he said, "HI, MOMMY." The nurse and I had tears in our eyes. His Aunt Sue and Uncle Thomas came to visit, and with them they brought a white Easter Bunny that was larger than Jack. He named it King Bunny. They were surprised but relieved to find Jack had made that much progress during the morning. Our family and the hospital staff were amazed how quickly he was coming back to life.

On Thursday night, the nurse suggested I lie in bed with Jack. He was dozing on and off most of the time. When he woke up this time, he began to engage in conversation. Prior to this illness, conversation was brief and strained. It seems the combination of viral meningitis and herpes encephalitis had caused him to speak slowly and methodically. Jack spoke without a stutter.

We talked of the events during the past few days, and then he said, "Mommy, I saw Nini, and she said I would be alright and then I saw Mary and she told me not to worry. I would be alright." My mother had passed away only eight months prior. We seldom spoke at home specifically about Mary, except in a Hail Mary prayer. I was impressed that Jack spoke of the details from his memory.

I asked, "What did Nini look like?"

Jack replied, "She looked like she always did before she was sick. Now she was wearing a white gown. Mary was wearing white and she had blue around her face. Her hair was brown and her eyes were blue." There was not a doubt in my mind that Jack was visited by Nini and Mary.

"Mommy, when I was really sick, before Nini and Mary came to see me in the hospital, there was this man poking me with a stick and it hurt." Jack must have been speaking about the doctor examinations and blood work.

Prayers are answered every day. Prayer groups from many Baptist, Methodist, and Catholic churches in central Florida and other states asked God to heal our son. An acquaintance was visiting a church in another town and heard our son's name mentioned. She wondered if this could be the same little boy that she knew. There is power in prayer. The more energy focused on prayer for someone in need does not go unnoticed. It was a miracle. If someone says God does not perform miracles anymore, then they just aren't looking with open eyes and hearts.

The following Monday, a week after our nightmare began, Jack was released from the hospital. The nurses took his picture to join the many others displayed on the wall near the nurses' station.

One nurse after another said, "You just don't know how rare it is to survive this kind of illness with little to no permanent disabilities."

The following week, Jack went to the neurologist at Nemours Children's Clinic for a follow-up exam.

After examining his eyes and coordination, the doctor remarked, "I wish I could take the credit. There really is no other explanation. This is a miracle." My husband and I gave each other a knowing look. We had been touched by the grace of God. We always had our faith in God. Now we experienced first-hand a miracle that medical science had no other explanation but to give God the credit.

After being home a month later, I was making devil ham sandwiches for a Mother's Day tea held at the preschool.

Jack grabbed the can of deviled ham and said, "Hey, this is the guy that was sticking me in the hospital!" The can has a solid red devil with horns holding a pitch fork. It wasn't the doctor after all.

We never spoke of the Devil to the children before this, which probably explains why he did not know his name. The last time I had made devil ham sandwiches was before Jack was born. I have been around children long enough to recognize when they are sincere. He never strayed from this story. By the time he became a teenager, he no longer remembered the details.

My advice to others is do not hesitate to ask God to help you, not just in a time of crisis but every day of your life. Hold your children close. One day they may not be with you. You may be powerless to act and be at the mercy of the Devil. The Devil wants to take souls. He will cause illnesses, nightmares, and accidents. My son has been the Devil's target the majority of his life. We will continue to support Jack in whatever manner is necessary. Each child is a precious gift from God that can never be replaced.

36

JOURNEY BACK TO CASSADAGA

After many years of resisting the temptation of seeking out mediums and psychics for guidance, I decided to attend a student mini reading psychic fair in Cassadaga, Florida in 1999. Our lives were back on track after Jack's brush with death. Mom left us in the summer of 1998, so I was long overdue for a checkup.

My resistance of psychics and mediums for this period of time was based on the influence of the Christian church. I wasn't convinced it was evil. In the Bible, Joseph and Solomon had prophetic dreams. The star of Bethlehem led the three wise men to Jesus. If the message is positive and helpful, why is it evil? I prayed to our Lord and asked him for guidance, forgiveness, and to protect our family every day.

I parked across the street from the community center. The old white-framed building had not changed, except for a gift shop located at the main entrance. When I walked into the building, the smell of incense could not be missed. Crystals, jewelry, and wind chimes were to the right of the entrance. Shelves of philosophy, religion, angel, and numerology books lined the walls in the rectangular shaped room. What is a Catholic doing in a place like this? I'm a Christian and should have no part of this, but I was driven to become more educated about my experiences. Traditional religion had not provided me with acceptable answers. I was on a spiritual quest. I reflected on a conversation I had with a Catholic spiritual friend. She told me spirituality does not originate from religion created by man, but spirituality emanates from the soul. I often reflect on our conversations. I have not seen my friend in many years, but she made an impact on my life.

I read the background of the readers participating in the psychic fair as I walked through the room. Student readers may be very general in their readings. You could walk away feeling robbed of your money. One woman in particular struck me as down to earth and sincere. She was a healer, and her husband a medium, so I felt the odds were in my favor she would prove to be accurate with detailed information. I was assigned a number and waited patiently to be called for my reading.

When it was my turn, I walked across the wood floors to the corner of the large open room. One half of the multipurpose room was divided by green screens and additional green screens were used to provide each medium/psychic a private area to give their reading. The medium was sitting beside a window. As I sat down at her card table, she asked me to say my first name and to hold her hands. She didn't hesitate but immediately began to speak of an elderly woman standing above and behind me.

The medium continued, "She says she is your grandmother and she is often with you. Although she crossed over when you were young, you were very close. She liked to cook." I was encouraged by this, but most grandmothers might fit this description. "She is bringing your father. He is doing a little dance, singing, and laughing. He has such a wonderful spirit. He has been to your home several times. He likes how you change the wreath on the front door during the different seasons of the year. He says you are doing a great job with your children. He has pink roses for you. Do you know what they symbolize?"

Well, I thought to myself, I've watched enough John Edwards Crossing Over shows to know it is a symbol of love. I nodded yes.

"I see a woman to your left side. Ssh. Ssh. Ssh. She is so overcome with emotion. I can't read you unless you calm down. She has not been gone very long, has she?"

"I didn't have to ask who this was. My mother would be overcome with emotion."

"She has been to visit you many times, but you know this. She says when she left her body, she found herself sitting on the front porch of the home she grew up in. Her mother was cooking her fried chicken. She says she is glad you have not gotten rid of her purses. She loved buying purses. Your mother is progressing, but it will take time to accept this transition to the level your father has obtained."

I left the camp feeling at peace that Mom was doing alright. I know my grandmother and dad were helping her adjust to this different way of existing on the other side. The communication from my parents and grandmother were messages of love.

It was a beautiful autumn day bringing relief from the hot days of summer; and yet my cheeks were beet red and the palms of my hands were itchy. At first I thought this is a fine time to begin hot flashes. I had little doubt these were symptoms when encountering the supernatural. I gratefully accepted this experience as a gift from God, not trickery from the dark side.

37

AURA WORKSHOP

Amy and I attended an aura workshop in February 2001. An aura is an illuminated field of a color or colors which radiate from an individual or an object. Amy had been seeing auras for a few years. She would use this ability to understand a classmate or teacher's feelings and personality. The workshop was an opportunity to learn more about our abilities.

It was held at the community building in Cassadaga. Many people were starting to gather. It was mostly women, but a few men participated. We chose our seats arranged in a semicircle.

The guest speaker was Reverend Steve Hermann. He bore a striking resemblance to the 1960's singer, Donovan, thick, curly dark brown hair and slender. He introduced basic information that auras vary by size, shape, and color for each person depending upon their physical health and spirituality. The aura maybe seen around the whole body. Modern technology can verify energy from the body as electromagnetic fields The group performed an exercise of meditation and concentration. A volunteer stood in front of the semicircle. While the group focused on the volunteer, they offered their impressions. The first was a professionally dressed petite woman. I was stunned to see an image similar to an old photo of a man and woman over her shoulder. In the past, I have heard other mediums give similar descriptions, now I was seeing it for the first time. I made the mistake of looking away and then looked back to find the image had vanished.

A middle age man volunteered for our exercise. My daughter volunteered to speak of a large energy field surrounding his body. The energy field of a short mother figure stood in front of him. Amy could feel the love this spirit had for her son. My daughter had tears in her eyes and spoke with a sweet motherly voice. There were small orbs surrounding the man as if to give him a group hug. One participant described the light as resembling a lighthouse beacon coming from above the volunteer. We were all touched by the love in this magical reading.

It was my turn to stand before the group. As the attention was focused on me, I began to feel warm. Maybe I felt self-conscious being put in the spotlight. I lost awareness of my own feelings as the participants gave their interpretations of what they saw surrounding me. A male participant saw a small scruffy white dog at my feet. I was asked if I had a dog fitting this description. I had taken care of my brother-in-law's dog who matched this description almost twenty years prior to this event. My daughter and two other women saw my aura but also saw the outline of a feminine body with large wings. The angel's aura or energy was sparkling with a glowing luminescent hue. A medium participating in the workshop said she saw an international gathering of spirit guides surrounding me. She felt the main spirit guide was an ancient Chinese man. My daughter saw many orbs moving around me. A petite grandmotherly figure with a large lace collar and her hair fashioned high off her neck pulled back from her face appeared behind me to one side. This possibly could be my maternal great-grandmother judging by the description. One of the men saw a rugged face elderly male wearing a western hat. My paternal grandfather and great-grandfather were from Texas. My grandfather had been a U. S. Marshall back in the days when marshals rode on horseback. My great-grandfather had a horse ranch in south Texas. I never met either of these grandparents, but the visions described by the group bore a close resemblance to family photos.

There was a variety of details seen in the aura workshop. Some people shared similar details, and others saw details not seen by fellow participants. I walked to my seat feeling weak, hot, tingly, and nauseous, not to mention that hot flash glow on my face.

I drove home feeling exhilarated. I was open for communication with the other side, but this experience was more than I could have ever hoped for. It was mind boggling to think I witnessed the sight of energy fields surrounding people, orbs flying around, and the faces of loved ones from the other side. I'm grateful for the information I gained from my daughter and the others who witnessed the spiritual activity around me.

Andrew Jackson Davis Educational Building, Cassadaga, Florida

38

GOD HAS A PLAN

In April 2001, I attended a psychic fair at the Andrew Jackson Davis Recreation Building in Cassadaga, Florida. I had one question that weighed heavily on my heart. My husband mentioned he was in pursuit of a relocation to Houston, Texas.

At first I would have welcomed the opportunity to live in another state, meet new people, and visit a variety of places we had never seen before. By this time in our lives, we had lived on the Space Coast for eighteen years. We lived less than an hour from where we grew up. Our children played and went to school with children they had known since birth. This was not welcomed news for me. Everywhere I went, I saw someone I knew. The sense of community gave me comfort. At this point in my life, my sense of adventure was nil.

I selected a medium/psychic that had been at the camp for quite some time. She had just been interviewed by one of the major cable networks. When my number was called to meet with the medium, I was directed to walk behind a solid green screen. Reverend Jean Sourant with a twinkle in her eye asked to hold my hands.

She said, "You are a day care or preschool director. I can tell because those who work with children and the elderly are doing work based on God's love." At that time, I was a preschool director.

Rev. Sourant said, "Your mother feels you were wise in changing stockbrokers and not to blame yourself. It could not have been expected, just ride it out and eventually the money will come back again." I was afraid my mother would blame me for the thousands of dollars I had lost in the stock market since March 2000. I have never paid too much attention to the stock market. My mother was obsessed with the market and read anything she could to be better informed. Mom never missed watching Louis Rukeyser's Wall Street Week on Friday nights. I was relieved to have that guilt removed.

The Reverend Sourant looked down at the card table and said, "I see a map with the state of Texas highlighted. You are moving to Texas, and it will happen this summer."

"Oh, no I don't want to move to Texas."

"Well, maybe you can stay in Florida and your husband can return home for visits, but it looks like you are moving, too."

I didn't relish the thought of living in a metropolitan area. It was not my wish for my children to grow up in that environment. I did not want to hear this prediction. I tried to put it in the back of my mind, but by May we traveled to Texas for my husband's interview. I knew he would be offered the job; the palms of my hands were itchy and tingled, a sign of an impending change. I was concerned the move would create a roadblock in my desire to gain more knowledge and understanding of the spirit world. I enjoyed adventure, but I did not want to leave my home and our roots in the community.

39

FIRST IMPRESSIONS

After we closed on the house, we stopped by our new home where the previous owners were waiting to go over a few of the mechanical points of the pool pump. We had a friendly visit. Just after they left, the smell of antiseptic and medicine wafted through the air. I asked my family if they could smell it. They said I was spooking them. Later my husband and oldest daughter confessed to recognizing the odor. The previous owner's son died five years earlier. He had melanoma and died in a hospital. I believe he was drawn to be with his parents as they said goodbye to their home of twenty-four years.

After moving into our new home, my husband and I were unpacking boxes. Paul called out from the bedroom. "Jane, your mom is here." The smell of roses filled the family room.

I said, "That's nice. She is checking out our new home in Texas. I have the feeling she approves."

My husband had returned to work and the children were in school within a few days of our move into the new home. One day I heard footsteps upstairs. The dog was outside. It was not the cats' pitter patter and scamper. I dismissed the creaks heard on the hardwood floor under the carpeting as the house settling. The third time it occurred, I could no longer ignore the footsteps.

I called upstairs, "Why don't you help clean up and unpack some boxes." The noise stopped. I guess ghosts and children both know how to escape household chores.

Shortly after we moved in, Amy was going to the cabana to shower. The cabana had a pool table, kitchen, and bathroom. She did not like sharing a bathroom with her siblings. The bathroom gave her privacy.

She opened the door to the building and heard a male voice say, "Don't forget to close the door."

She replied, "I always close the door. Now leave me alone." The voice did not respond. My husband also has heard in the cabana, a male making a heavy sigh.

While I was refinishing kitchen cabinets in our carport, I noticed a transparent figure of a young man, tall and lean, light-colored hair dressed in khaki slacks and a button-down short-sleeve madras shirt, walking across our court. The man dematerialized as he stepped onto the grass.

Amy was in her bedroom when something caught her attention out of the corner of her eye. She quickly turned to the bedroom door and saw only the face of a young man with sandy blond hair. He was looking directly at her, then disappeared.

Rachel was walking down the stairs of our home. At about midway, she saw at the bottom of the stairs the face of the young man peeping around the doorway. When she reached the bottom of the stairs, there was no sign of him.

Several years later, a neighbor was walking by our house while I was doing yard work. She greeted me with a friendly hello. We began to chat for a brief time, then out of the blue she asked me if I had seen the ghost of a young man who wore khaki pants and a sixties style madras shirt. I confirmed my family had seen him inside and outside of our home. How reassuring to know we aren't the only ones who have supernatural experiences.

40

REGRESSION

After the move half way across the nation, it took some time for me to unpack and set up our new home and re-establish a routine. When the dust finally settled, I began to return to chronicling my family's encounters. Regression was the next step to understanding my experiences. It was my preference to meet with a regressionist who I felt comfortable. Since the move to Houston, my search for a better understanding of my dreams of a pass life led me oddly enough back to the old Florida that I knew best, less than a mile from my childhood home.

One of the first regression websites that popped up on the internet was Dr. Dan Baldwin. The website seemed to answer many of my questions. After I read his article, his address appeared in small print at the bottom of the page. I don't believe in coincidences. It was amazing that I would find a regressionist over a thousand miles away residing near the rural community where I grew up.

In the spring of 2002, my husband was asked to travel back to Kennedy Space Center for business. This was a wonderful opportunity to visit friends and have a regression. Locating the Baldwin's geodesic contemporary home off of the one lane county road was easy. I had traveled down that road thousands of times while growing up in central Florida. I was greeted by a friendly distinguished gentleman. When we walked into the house, I was asked to take my shoes off at the door. My mom and dad also had that rule. Unfortunately I've never been able to influence my husband to accept this practice.

He led me through the large open entrance. Mrs. Baldwin was on the phone seated at a desk in the reception area. Large vibrant colored paintings hung from the white walls. By this time his wife was off the phone, walked toward us, and greeted me with a smile. She was equally as warm as her husband. They offered me a bottle of water, and we walked upstairs to their office. I sat on a long sofa, which was against the wall. They sat in two chairs to the left of me. We discussed my recurring dreams and concerns about being regressed.

I asked, "How will I know that I am just not making up things in my head?" She explained when you are regressed the images and words come to you. You are in a very relaxed state. You are aware of your surroundings, but you are an observer. They taped the session of which I received a copy. My recorded account is often fragmented. I have written the statements in more complete sentences for clarity.

"You are interested in your past lives."

"Ever since I was a child, I would witness myself as an adult in recurring dreams." I resembled the woman in my dreams: short, fair complexion, dark hair. Before we began, I recounted attending a quilting class in my present life. The instructor demonstrated how to make a running stitch and to insert the needle in the batting leaving the knot at the end of the thread within the batting. It was natural for me as if I had been quilting for years.

"We will focus on the memories that you have. Hypnosis uses an induction. When you begin to talk and ask questions, your awareness starts to shift. Consciousness shift depends on what is going on and shift into a deeper and altered state. It is like any other art form. It is a practice and not a science. It is not the work of the Devil. Your goal is to explore, some type of validation."

I counted backwards from ten to one. My eyes were closed, my body relaxed in a sitting position. Another recurring dream depicted me driving down a road. It was at night on an old two-lane bridge with supports framed from up above. As I crossed the bridge, the car felt like it was beginning to fall into the dark water. A part of the bridge had washed away. There was nothing I could do to prevent it. All I could see was black water with the reflection of the car lights. Every time I had this dream, I would wake up before going into the water.

"You did not want to be attached to the car."

"Oh, this is the car. It is in 1908. Katherine went over the bridge."

"In that alter state edit is rare and rare that we lie. It is an honest state. Say a prayer. We are here only to be helpful and harmless without exception. We will be healed as you chose us to be healed. Spark of God consciousness in our center. Eternal and destructible. Feel it as it spreads throughout your body, emanating from that spark, the center. Imagine the light spreading out in many directions, arms spreading out. Protected and shield within that bubble of light. The bubble of light glows like a light bulb. And that bubble of light glows within. The entire surrounding area surrounded and filled with that light from that spark of God consciousness. As you focus inward, you have told us about your memories. These were at the top of your head but came for some reason. Describe what image comes, a scene, a face, a physical sensation, anything from a starting point."

"I don't know if I am trying too hard."

"Say these words. I just want to know more. Say it again. Recall another time and another place. I want to understand and know more and trust what comes. We are not judging and analyzing. We just want to understand what comes. Do you feel any sensation?"

"I feel lightheaded and see the color purple. My eyes are blinking."

"You have entered the alpha state. Focus on the purple. Where does it take you?"

"I'm sitting in a buggy. Images begin to appear in a flash. Like in a movie. I am driving the buggy and I am out in the open. The buggy has a canopy with fringe around the edge."

"Horses?"

"I see my hands holding the reins. It is a lacy glove, but my fingers are showing. I have a dark dress on. It is daytime."

"Warm or cold?"

"The temperature was comfortable, neither warm nor cold."

"Do you see anyone?"

"I am passing the house. It is two storied. I see some screening and there is a gate. I see a little picket fence. There are trees to the left of me. There is one horse. It is a dark horse."

"What is your destination?"

"I am alone. I am going to see a friend."

"Trust that knowing."

"I am moving on."

"What is your emotional tone?"

"I am calm."

"How old are you?"

"I have dark hair."

"What is your name?"

"The name that comes to mind is Polly." I don't believe this is my name but the lady's name.

"Trust what comes. You are doing just fine. What happens next?"

"I see a brick house. I have parked and I'm getting out of the buggy. It is on an incline. It has a porch on the side. I am walking toward the porch. There is a lady who comes to the door. She is an older lady and kind of heavy set. She is happy to see me. I give her a hug."

"What happens next?"

"She is walking me through the back door. I am in a kitchen. She has on a long apron and her hair is in a bun. I am taking off my hat. I am dressed up. I have a lacy shawl on my shoulders. I am not as old as I am now. I know her, but I really don't."

"Tell what you see without Jane's input. Without Jane's comparison. Leave that behind."

"I see stairs. I see a grandfather clock."

"What is her connection?"

"She owns her house. I didn't go through the front. It is statelier. I went through the back. I know her really well. I don't need to come through the front. I don't think she's my mom. I feel that she is a relative."

"What is the purpose? Is it friendly or has some purpose?"

"I didn't bring anything."

"Have you visited on other occasions?"

"I am familiar with her. She was waiting on me. She knew I was coming."

"Skip forward to the next most important thing that happens."

"I was sitting down in the kitchen having tea."

"What happens next?"

"She is sitting with me. I am worried about her health. She seems fine. Her cheeks are really rosy. She has fair skin with the veins near the surface. She is asking about somebody, but I don't know who."

"How are the boys?"

"She knows your family."

"They are the same as usual. There really is not much of a purpose."

"What are the thoughts beneath the surface?"

"She is quite a bit older than me. I think she works too hard. She has a nice house. Somehow she feels she has to do it all. I don't think I have to work as hard as she does. Her kids are all gone. I don't see her husband around. She maintains the house. She does not have any help."

"What happens next?

"A man is coming in. He is kind of thin with a boney face. He gives me a hug. He is tired and old. He is her husband. I think I know them from church. I like to visit people. They seem happy to see me. She is a lot bigger than he is. He is older than her."

"Skip forward to a significant event. You have a friendly connection."

"I am standing in a cemetery. I feel so sad."

"Who has died?"

"I am not sure." I know it was a family member, but it is too painful to think about.

"Look around you. Are there other people standing around?"

"There are a lot of people and the men have tall hats. I have a black hanky. There are black buggies lined up all along the road. I think people are with me."

"My buggy is creamy and has fringe on it. Someone is getting into the back seat. A man is getting in alongside me. There are children in the backseat."

"Who is this man to you?

"He is my husband. He has a black hat and a beard. I don't know why, but I have tears in my eyes. We are just driving away. The last thoughts as I drive away. I am very fortunate and have a good life. Someone wants to come to the house. I don't want him to come. It is a man. He just wants to talk to my husband. I'll excuse myself and go to my room."

"Skip forward to a major significant event in that life time."

"There is a wedding."

"What do you say to each other?"

"There is light coming in through the window. I think I have a daughter. My daughter is getting married. She is wearing white, and it is a very elaborate dress. She is taller than me. She is tall like her father."

"Is your hair still black?"

"No, there are strands of white. I wear a hat to hide it. I don't like gray hair."

"What is happening on this wedding day?"

"I am in a bedroom. She is happy, and I am sad. There are layers and layers of fabric. I am giving her advice. I think she is listening but not really listening."

"Are you happy with the man she is marrying?"

"Skip forward to the end of the ceremony."

"It is bringing me to tears. I don't know if I trust him that much. He is short, and she is taller."

"Does something bother you about him?"

"He is an opportunist. I am reserving judgment. She is so happy. Wisely I don't blurt it out. It would only make her mad. She has to find out on her own. Maybe I am wrong."

"Skip forward."

"She had a baby. I am happy."

"How does it feel to be a grandmother?"

"I am worried. She looks good. She is wearing a pretty nightgown. And her hair is up."

"Are you worried about her, or you have never trusted him."

"He is standing behind me. He seems happy. She is handing me the baby."

"As you take the baby, what thoughts come?"

"The baby has pretty black hair like me and blue eyes. I am giving the baby to him. I don't want to be too greedy."

"The look on his face?"

"He is really proud. He seems to be supportive. He seems to have been a good provider."

"Skip forward to the last day of your life. Where are you indoors or outdoors?"

"I am inside, in bed."

"Are there other people with you?"

"There are young adults."

"Is your husband there?"

"I don't like them all gawking at me."

"Is your hair all white?"

"I have a cap on. I am old. My body feels tired and old, but I'm not actually that old in age."

"How has your life been?"

"It has been good. It is a comfortable life."

"As you take your last breath, what are your last thoughts?"

"I am very loved. They hate to see me go. I feel myself going up."

"Any promises you made to your daughter and your grandchildren? Were there any promises made to your husband?"

"No, I don't remember making any promises to my husband."

"I am confused about when he died. He was by my bedside when I died in that life all so long ago. Yet now he is coming to greet me. He looks like he did when we first met, thick black hair, fair skin, wearing a long sleeve white button-down shirt with black slacks. I didn't like losing my looks. I look like I use to."

"Look into his eyes. The vibration in his eyes, the windows of the soul. Look into your daughter's eyes. It is not the appearance of the face. Feel the vibration. Feel her essence and her vibration. The windows of the soul."

"I don't feel as close to her as I do my daughter Amy. I love her."

The confusion of love ones and emotions from different lives leaves me in a quandary.

"We come back often as a soul family. We take on different roles. Anything that would hold you to that life?"

"Not really. I like my furnishings."

"I stand up from my cane back and seat rocker. I've been so weak. It has been difficult to breathe for a while. I had no body strength to stand up and walk, but now I can. Before I go, I will walk through my beautiful home that I love so much. One of my favorite pieces in the bedroom is my empire dresser. I walked past the dresser, headed to the door to say a final farewell to my home. No one sees me walk past them. It is a strange, eerie feeling. I am going to miss my life. I am happy."

"How does it feel when he takes your hand?"

"It is very nice. He says it is about time. Step across into the white light."

"It is so bright. It is like walking into the sun, but it doesn't burn you up. It doesn't hurt your eyes. This is home for a little while."

"How does that feel?"

"It feels good."

"You were loved that is all you really need."

"Play no dido. Want to explore that one?"

"I am all by myself. My husband is not with me."

"Which life is it now?"

"I am trying to think. Those boys. I am having to handle those boys. It seems the room is lighter and airier."

"What color is your skin?"

"Oh, I am white."

"Is this your house? What is your clothing like?"

"A long dress."

"The fabric heavy or light?"

"It is taffeta. It is late afternoon. Somebody is coming. And those boys are giving me problems. They know I mean business. Now they are leaving me, and now I sigh. I feel a bit better. I have things to do."

"What happens next?"

"I am telling somebody to do something."

"What color is her skin?"

"She is black. It is a young servant girl. I like her a lot. She is a real good girl. She needs to do something in the dining room with the condiments. Relatives are coming. I like them. I am happy about it. They brought a trunk. It is not just for dinner."

"What are they to you?"

"My sister is coming. She is bringing her husband."

"Is there anyone else? Skip forward to the moment they arrive."

"I am happy to see them. I greet them. There is a little girl. She is holding her mother's hand and a little doll in her other hand. I'm thinking I wish my husband was here. I am sad about it. He is not here. I know he is not coming."

"Skip back to the last time you saw him."

"He is getting on a train."

"Are you there wishing him on?"

"He is hanging on the long silver handle by the step. He says he loves me and he will miss me. I don't want him to go. I don't like it one bit. I don't like being home with the kids."

"It is a lot to handle by yourself."

"He is very good-looking and well-dressed."

"Where is he going on this day? For what purpose? To a big city?"

"He is going to buy something. He is not a farmer. He is not a rancher. He is a business man."

106

"What happens? Move forward. Describe what happens."

"I have a telegram. He won't be back. He is caught up in something."

"What does the telegram say? What is the message?"

"A shipment did not come in. He has to inspect a shipment. They're in big crates. He can't come home until everything is in from a factory."

"Is he at that factory while your sister is there?"

"I am so angry."

"Skip forward to your visit."

"The boys are nice there. They play with her real well. I feel bad her husband doesn't have a man to talk to. But I can't do anything about it. He is friendly, but he doesn't get involved in our chit chat."

"How long will their visit be?"

"Longer than a week but not quite a month. My husband is coming home at the end of their visit. He comes home and takes off his hat. I am happy. The boys run in to see him. Her husband is happy to see him. He is tired of us women."

"Skip to the most important part of that life. The event by which the most important part of that life is shaped."

"I don't know. I think he is gone."

"Who is gone?"

"My husband is gone. Is he traveling or left this life? I don't think he is coming back. I have a lot of business to deal with."

"What happened to change your life? Something tells me he was in a train accident. Maybe I am trying too hard. I don't know if he is coming back."

"How old are the boys?"

"They are preteens. One has overalls on, more youthful play wear. One boy is older. He is supportive and seems to know what is going on. He feels he has to be the man of the house. He is pretty respectful."

"In that time, what is your name?"

"Elizabeth came into my mind. I didn't hear anyone call my name."

"Skip forward to the last day of your life."

"I don't think I am really old. I think I became ill."

"Can you feel your body? Can you feel the illness?"

"I am weak. Are you ready to leave that life?"

"The boys, how old are they now?"

"Young men."

"Is there anything holding you?"

"I am too tired. It is okay if I go."

"Don't play no dido. Is it a good memory?"

"They got into something and took it. They were not thinking. They know how I want everything to be just right. They know I am tense. I guess they thought it was funny. I don't think it was funny."

"Now you are at the end of your life and you're tired."

"I still have dark hair. I am middle aged. I got over it. It's not important, seemed that way at the time."

"Watch yourself come out of the body. Where are you?"

"I am standing in front of it."

"What decisions are you making?"

"I am thinking. I can now move around. I am slumped over in the wheel chair."

"What are you doing now?"

"I am walking around. It is pretty carpeting. I don't see anybody. I don't feel quite like going. Someone is calling me. I better go."

"Where are they?"

"They are far away. It is time to go to heaven. Their voices are stronger. It is like a swish."

"Do you recognize anyone there?"

"Yes, my husband."

"What is the feeling?"

"We could have had a nice life together. That is okay. What is done is done. My grandma is there. I am happy to see her."

"Reach out your hand. Who takes your hand?"

"Grandma. I've hugged my husband."

"We change roles from earlier times."

"I am looking down at this couple. There is trouble. Temperamental. I'm not sure I want to go."

"Who was she?

"She has the eyes of the lady I went to visit. She had a hard time in this life. She does her best. She needs me."

"You were her friend in another time. Now you can be her friend again."

"If she would let me. It is her lesson. She didn't learn it until it was finally at the end. A lot of ups and downs. Her husband was a mischievous boy. He was always getting into trouble."

"What have you have come together to experience?"

"We are a lot alike. We like nature. We like people. We like music."

"What is the purpose of coming together as Jane?"

"What is the purpose? Love. Compassion. Caring."

"Did you achieve it?"

"Yes."

"Took more time with my mother."

"Look around in the planning stage. Can you find them in the light? Amy, Rachel, Jack."

"I recognized her (Amy) even before you said that. People come to her. She is a pure spirit. She gives and gives. She seems to glow. We used to work together."

"The purpose of coming together?"

"We just like each other so much. We like to be together. Little Jack. He has always seemed to be a little boy."

"What is the purpose?"

"He likes me being his mother. I'll make him into a good person. Rachel. She is a real sweetheart. She is spoiled. She has never been a grown up with me."

"What have we planned for this life together?"

"She needs to give of herself. Giving and receiving of herself. It will take time. She won't realize until she grows up. I feel like crying."

"Where do the tears take you?"

"Challenges. The unknown. And Paul."

"In the planning stage have you known him before? Do you recognize him, his vibration?"

"He is always working, but he comes back. He likes to be protective. He likes to be the worker. He gets frustrated with me. I like to have control over things, too. He backs away. I feel nauseous."

"Where do you feel it in the body?"

"In my throat and chest."

"If they could speak in words, what would the words be saying?"

"I don't know. It is not pleasant."

"Is there something significant? Who brings this nausea?"

"Hard times."

"Who says hard times? Is this part of Jane?"

"No, it is not Jane."

"What are you doing here with Jane?"

"She has been through hard times. She had to work to keep things going. Grow food. Couldn't shop. I am Jane, but now I am not. It is me. We are one and the same. She is always appreciative. She would never want to go back to that."

"Is there another lingering feeling of the hard times?"

"In the mind. Want to be comfortable. Not ever want to be hungry."

"How does that make Jane feel?"

"There is always food on the table. No one ever wants for anything. One time she had to dig and grow food. It was so hard."

"When was that, that she had to live like that? Another time and place?"

"Yes."

"What was the purpose of you coming up now?"

"I don't want her to forget. I need those hard times. She has never had to go back."

"You have the memory. How old was Jane when you found her?"

The voice of the entity was soft and very child-like.

"We have been together how long? She was little. I am confused. It is confusing. My head is spinning. I have never felt this way before."

"What is your name? How old were you when you died? You bring forward nausea and hard times. Jane is thinking and you are trying to protect?"

"Always looking for water and looking for everything."

"What calendar year is it?"

"1863."

"What color is your skin?"

"White."

"Recall the last day. How old are you?"

"I am little. Five."

"What did you do when you came out of that body? How did that body die?"

"Any food?"

"I am what you call neglected. My name is Suzie."

"It is brave to come out and leave those hard times. Did you look up? Look up, and what do you see?"

"Twinkles. Close and far away. Twinkles far away. Closer."

"You can leave the nausea of that neglect. Be sure you gather all your parts and pieces to the light. There will be no more hunger or thirst."

"I feel better now."

"Who were the twinkles?"

"Helpers."

"I've been gone a long time."

"Goodbye."

"Jane said she didn't mean any harm."

"Clear any residue. Confusion, tears, fears, hunger, rescue spirits of life."

"Jane is looking better now."

"I feel a lot better now."

"Is there anybody else there? Anyone? Mercy band and rescue angel band of light. Clean up band of teams of light. How does that feel? Any messages from your mother or father?"

"He thinks I have done a good job. He will watch over Jack. I am tired. I feel hazy. So much at one time. Over load."

"You were deeply altered."

My hands and neck were in the same position for hours. My neck leaned on my right shoulder. If I knew I was going to be in this state for so long, I would have lied down. I was so stiff after almost four hours of regression.

I thought about how as a child I never felt full. My mother would say not to snack before dinner because it would spoil my meal. It never spoiled my meal. It has always been a struggle to maintain my weight. It has been easier to control my appetite since Suzie left my body.

The Baldwins explained the spirits of humans and demons can attach themselves to people. The spirits can wander in a state of confusion, unaware what has happened to them. Suzie wandered earthbound for over 100 years. She died during the Civil War, abandoned and alone. Her spirit became attached to me when I was a child.

Past life regression should be guided by someone who is trained. This is an intense experience not to be left in the hands of someone dabbling in hypnosis. It is a deep introspective look at yourself and those who deeply touch our lives. Souls reincarnate touching one another dynamically within the family and their circle of friends. I felt physically frozen during the regression. I walked away elated and light headed with a greater sense of who I am and where I have been.

41

MYRTLES PLANTATION

In October of 2001, my family traveled to Natchez, Mississippi for the Annual Fall Pilgrimage of antebellum homes. On the return drive back to Houston, we decided to tour the Myrtles Plantation in Francisville, Louisiana. I had seen the plantation on the Travel Channel. It is not only historically well-known, but it's perhaps one of the most haunted homes in the U.S.

On the day of our visit, the sky was overcast. The autumn leaves were scattered on the driveway and lawn. Crepe myrtles on the grounds no longer held their blooms. Although the plantation home had many windows and wide hallways to allow cross ventilation, it did seem dark and a bit oppressive.

The home is a residence and a bed and breakfast. Legend tells of the untimely death of a mother and her two daughters who were accidentally poisoned by a slave named Chloe. Chloe prepared a cake laced with poisonous oleander leaves with the intent to nurse the mother and children back to health to secure her place as a house servant rather than be sent to work in the fields. Unfortunately she was heavy handed on the oleander, resulting in their deaths.

As we toured the home, our group moved into the living room. Amy and I were standing with our backs toward a corner. The scent of lilacs wafted by me.

I whispered, "Amy, do you smell lilacs in the corner?" She refused to place herself in such proximity because she could smell it from where she was standing. The guide later mentioned in her dialogue that the mistress of the house was known for her lilac perfume.

I was one of the first to walk into the dining room before the others gathered around a large rectangular dining room table. There were two chandeliers. The one closest to me began to tilt to the right. Only one of the chandelier arms visibly vibrated. It looked as if someone was touching it by only one light bulb.

I commented, "Oh, oh, while others also witnessed this unusual sight."

There is a story pertaining to a large mirror in the entrance. It is across from a grand staircase. The mirror was not covered at the time of the mother and daughters' funeral. This ritual of covering mirrors is practiced in Jewish, Hindu, and Catholicism faiths. Folklore passed down through generations explains the soul of the deceased may become trapped in the mirror, or since the angel of death is present for the deceased, the soul of someone visiting the home maybe taken shortly thereafter, if their reflection is in the mirror.

The silver of the mirror at the Myrtles Plantation fades but not due to age. The silver has been replaced several times, but finger prints appear with regular occurrence. It is believed to be from the other side. Cleaning the mirror has not been the solution. The guide mentioned photos taken of the mirror may develop images of those from another time. I did take a photo without much thought that something would develop. Shortly after our return to Houston, the photo did indicate the shadow of a well-groomed man in a period suit. My husband became a believer. He enlarged the print. Clearly this was tangible proof to us that another dimension exists in the shadows.

By the time the tour had ended, I felt so nauseous. My chest was tight, as if someone was standing on me. After leaving the plantation, it was at least thirty minutes before this feeling left me. The Myrtles Plantation was the most haunted site I have ever visited during the day. I have no desire to spend the night. If the Myrtles Plantation is on your bucket list of haunted homes to visit, I encourage you to take the tour. You will not be disappointed.

Haunted mirror at the Myrtles Plantation

42

BEDROOM INTRUDER

Rachel's room in our Texas home was always colder than any other room in the house. When she would go to sleep with her blankets wrapped around her as tight as a cocoon, she would wake up with them pulled down to the footboard. Some nights she would wear a hooded sweatshirt and socks. In the morning, she would find herself with the socks and hoodie folded neatly laying by her pillow.

Occasionally at night, we could hear the sound of furniture moving in her upstairs bedroom. She had wall to wall carpeting, yet it was the sound of furniture being pulled along a hardwood floor. We would go upstairs to investigate, but nothing looked out of the ordinary.

On one occasion, she woke up by the sound of drawers opening and closing. There was a young man rummaging through the desk. He appeared solid but faded. She sat up in bed to see more clearly. He was tall, slender, wearing belted dress slacks, a small patterned button-down shirt, and underneath a white t-shirt. His brown hair was tussled.

Rachel asked, "Why are you going through my desk drawers?"

The spirit in a frantic voice said, "The papers!"

He continued to frantically search. She lay back down in bed and covered her head with the blankets, eventually falling back to sleep. Why didn't she run out of her bedroom to get someone? I believe we have experienced so many encounters; our family accepts it as a nuisance, but nothing to fear.

43
SPIRIT'S WISDOM

Rachel, as a child, was always faithful in her nightly prayers to God. Since we moved to Texas, she prayed not to be afraid of spirits. One night she received the answer to her prayers. She dreamed of being in a dark room. The interior walls were constructed of horizontal wooden slats. An elderly Native American woman was sitting in a primitive wooden rocking chair. She had a pattern blanket wrapped around her shoulders and wore a dress that reached her feet. Her gray hair was in a single braid. Her almond-shaped brown eyes and high cheekbones were aglow. There were no visible windows, lamps, or candles.

The old woman called, "Rachel."

Rachel asked, "Who are you?"

She replied, "Your spirit guide. Rachel, don't be afraid of spirits. They are just as afraid as you are. Some don't know they are dead. Remember, they were once living."

Rachel remembers this being the extent of her dream. She felt very comforted by the words of this spirit guide.

44

I MISS YOU

In May of 2002, a love from a former life came to visit me in a dream. It appeared that I was gliding in a very large space. The area felt as if there was a ceiling, floor, and walls, but I could not see them. As I began to move, the sensation was similar to skating without moving my legs, as if gliding in an invisible space of soft white light. I was laughing and enjoying myself with other people, who along with me wore flowing white garments lacking any detail. Their faces did not look familiar to me.

A man was standing in the distance. He appeared to be in his thirties, medium built in stature, and looked French. My husband, Paul, is 6' 3" and of German descent. Compared to Paul, the love from a bygone era was somewhat short in height. He looked familiar dressed in a black pair of slacks and white button-down long-sleeved shirt with one or two buttons left undone around the collar. He had black, thick, wavy hair, chestnut brown eyes, fair complexion, and a long narrow nose and a pronounced line crossed his forehead. He was looking directly at me and smiling. As I moved closer to him, feelings came to me of a life so long ago, a life filled with love and happiness.

His hand reached for mine, and together we glided effortlessly through the space. No words were exchanged. We communicated with our thoughts and touch. I was overwhelmed with the love I had for him and he for me. We were together once again I moved behind him, my arms tightly wrapped around his waist. This embrace felt like no other. I deeply inhaled the back of his neck, consumed by the love we once shared. I remember thinking I want this experience to never end. I wanted to always remember his smell and touch.

Just as soon as I began to exhale, my mind was flooded with the thoughts of my children in my current life. They couldn't grow up without me. How could I abandon them? Did I have a choice to stay with him and never return to my current life? It was not an option to remain in this heavenly state. I found myself being pulled backward landing in my bed. I woke up startled. It felt like a dream, but maybe, it was an astral projection.

Some people may believe this was only an imaginary tale experienced only in a dream state. For the next few months, my mind was preoccupied with this dream. It was beautiful and melancholy at the same time. I was overcome with emotion, and tears would well up in my eyes whenever I thought of him. The details are just as vivid as the night of my dream. A return visit from him would feel bitter sweet. I must focus on today and not what was in the past. When the day arrives that I'm called home, I wish for this former love to greet me.

45

GREAT BALL OF FIRE

Rachel was watching television in the family room one spring day in 2002. It was a Saturday afternoon, and the rest of the family left for a few hours to watch Jack's baseball game.

She heard a rumble outside and looked up toward the large picture window. The sky was blue without a cloud in sight. While Rachel was seated in a chair beside the window, a somewhat round shaped solid object varying in shades of dark blue, light blue, and glowing white light zoomed through the window to the center of the room and abruptly stopped. The window remained intact.

Rachel felt the room grow warmer as the object expanded. Once it stopped expanding, it abruptly vanished. The room became cooler almost instantly. She was relieved to have the family return from the baseball game.

Balls of light normally occur when there has been an electrical storm. It is a rare occurrence. The light seemed to have intelligence. Many documented incidences have been witnessed by others. I wish I knew why this spectral ball of light entered our family room than disappeared.

46

DAD'S PHOTO

While going through old family photos, I discovered a picture of my father sitting at the piano. It is the same piano I have in my home today. I planned to purchase a frame, so I left the photo out on my bedroom dresser.

Amy said early one morning before going to school, "Do you smell cigarette smoke?"

Hurriedly I replied, "No." I was busy cooking my son's breakfast. I was intent on getting his meal ready and not thinking about another paranormal experience. After preparing his meal, I went into my bedroom and smelled the burning cigarette. I believe our love ones who have crossed over feel comforted by our thoughts of them as we honor their memory with photos and mementos displayed in our homes. Dad was letting Amy and I know he was with us.

47

GRAY MIST

Our family was planning to vacation in Mountain Home, Arkansas in June of 2002. I had been busy washing clothes, ironing, and packing for the five of us. I liked to set my ironing board in the family room and iron while watching T.V.

One morning while ironing, I noticed movement out of the corner of my left eye. I turned and saw a light gray cloud approximately two feet long and one foot in depth swirling toward one of the ceiling's corners by the doorway leading from the family room into the living room. I put the iron down and watched. The apparition was probably present for less than a minute, but it seemed longer. It floated and swirled into the ceiling. I ran upstairs to see if it came through the floor, but I saw no evidence of its presence. This was before iPhones came to be available on the market. Where is the camera when you need it?

48

EUREKA SPRINGS

In the summer of 2002, my family and I vacationed in the Ozark Mountains. We discovered the Victorian town of Eureka Springs. This jewel of a town has changed little during the last century. In the nineteenth century, wealthy northern families would travel by train to experience the springs for their medicinal qualities.

My husband and I picked up a brochure advertising ghost tours in The Crescent Hotel. The tour guide escorted the groups throughout the building, giving a historical account of the past century. In the 1930's, a road show medicine man by the last name of Baker purchased the hotel which had fallen on hard times due to the depression. He misrepresented himself as a physician. He claimed he could cure cancer. He manipulated the wealthy to continue their stay convalescing and to send letters to their families to arrange for money to be wired to the clinic to continue their treatments. Many patients succumbed to their terminal illnesses, unbeknownst to their relatives, yet the money continued to be wired to pay for their loved one's medical services.

During our tour, many participants experienced malfunctions of their cameras. As we walked through the halls known for their frequency of spiritual activity, newly purchased batteries were drained of their energy. Smoking was not permitted in the halls, but the smell of cigarette smoke permeated around the group. Many of those present acknowledged the smell. We especially enjoyed this tour because it wasn't theatrical. We vowed we would return to The Crescent Hotel.

A year and a half later, we celebrated our wedding anniversary at The Crescent. I came prepared this time with a digital tape recorder and Gauss EMF detector and my 35 mm camera loaded with 800 speed film. We stayed in room twenty. Apparitions had appeared in this room for previous guests. I would linger in the halls hoping to catch a glimpse of supernatural activity. I didn't see or experience a thing.

My husband, on the other hand, did not go with the hope of spotting a ghost. He was there for the wedding anniversary. While walking down the hall near our room, he saw a nurse dressed in a traditional white uniform with white hose and shoes walk through a wall into a room. The morning of our departure while getting off the elevator, he came face to face with a transparent, older gentlemen dressed in a dark suit and black top hat.

Paul said, "Good morning." The man tipped his hat and continued to walk a few more steps through the lobby, than dematerialized. Paul mentioned the experience to the desk clerk. The clerk confirmed that in the nineteenth century, a doctor had his office in the hotel. He was known to dress in a dark suit and a top hat. A picture of the doctor is displayed in the elevator.

We did enjoy ourselves. The ghost hunting part of the trip was not in vain. I wish I had evidence, but a first-hand account from my husband was good enough for me.

The Crescent Hotel, Eureka Springs, Arkansas

49

NATHAN

My husband's parents had been married for sixty-two years. During the last nine months of their time together, Nathan was fighting pancreatic, lung, and brain cancer. Paul's mother, Vivian, would not speak of Nathan's impending death. She didn't want him to give up. Sixty-two years is a lot of time to be together. As Christians we know God calls us to come home when it is our time. He has prepared a place for us. We will be reunited with family and friends. There will be no pain and suffering. As reassuring as that maybe, it is difficult to accept the end is near.

Three months after the death of Nathan, we visited my mother-in-law, Vivian. Several members of the family later met for dinner. When we returned to her home, we parked the car in the garage and entered through the kitchen door. Before I stepped into the kitchen, I heard someone whistling. My husband also heard the tune. Vivian acknowledged she heard something but gave an explanation of it being the pipes. I had never heard the pipes whistle. No water had been turned on. She did seem to have a smile on her face. Nathan was known to whistle from time to time. Do mechanical household fixtures change pitch and make a rhythmic tune? By the time we walked into the living room, the whistling had stopped. The whistle did not return for the duration of our visit.

50

SOMEONE'S WATCHING OVER ME

One afternoon at the beginning of Rachel's sophomore year in high school, she was walking across the courtyard on her way to the school bus loop. She noticed in her peripheral vision the outline of wings. When she turned her head, she saw a high school age young man dressed in jeans, a dark knit T-shirt, and black overcoat down to his knees. He was wearing dark sunglasses, but unlike a typical teenager, he had huge, brilliant white wings extend below his overcoat.

He was standing around a small group of students but not actively engaged in their conversation. It appeared they were not aware of his presence. Although he was wearing sunglasses, Rachel seemed to feel he was very aware of her noticing him. She quickly looked away. When she looked again, he was still standing in the same location minus the wings. She felt his eyes continue to watch her as she walked toward the buses.

Once she reached her destination, Rachel and a girlfriend sat toward the back of the bus. Both girls noticed the odor of something burning. They looked around, but nothing seemed out of the ordinary. A few seconds later, smoke was billowing out from under their seats. They called out to the bus driver who immediately directed all of the students to exit the bus.

School administrators and security interrogated students at length to determine who was responsible for setting a mop on fire. A male student chose to commit this potentially dangerous inappropriate act out of boredom. I can't help but think the angel was watching over the students.

51

A PENNY FROM HEAVEN

My husband was sent on a business trip to St. Louis, Missouri in July 2005. He had worked for an aerospace contractor for the past twenty-five years. It was rare that our family had an opportunity to travel with him. We decided to drive and make it our summer vacation trip.

Unfortunately for Paul, he would not be able to sightsee once he began work in St. Louis. Rachel, Jack and I left early one morning and drove to Springfield, Illinois, to tour the home and museum of Abraham Lincoln. Thanks to my father, I have a life-long love for history. Whenever the opportunity arises, I arrange family trips to historical sites. It pleases me to say the children have inherited this appreciation of the past and the knowledge we can learn from its history.

It was a beautiful summer day. Perfect for hundreds of school age children and families to tour the historic district. Abraham Lincoln's home was the main attraction. We walked from room to room of this great man's residence, impressed by the small desk where he spent endless hours writing. While we grasped the banister of his home's staircase, we thought of the countless times he had grasped that same railing. Everyone on the tour respectfully listened to the words of the guide.

After the tour was completed, we decided to visit the Lincoln Museum. It would do us good to walk instead of hunting for another parking space closer to the museum. We walked for several blocks. At one point, we were alongside a concrete, modern building. There was an overhang extending almost completely over the wide sidewalk.

As we were walking, a small dark object jettisoned diagonally from the ceiling on our right and struck Rachel on her right shoulder. We heard it hit the pavement. If you were to look up, all you would see would be solid concrete. There were no windows or openings along the side wall. There was no other object on the sidewalk but a copper-plated penny. The three of us stared at one another in disbelief. Where did it come from? We looked closely above us. There were no holes, no grating. It just appeared out of thin air. I picked up the penny and examined the date....1973, the year my father died.

I said, "Kids, we are not alone. My dad's enjoying the trip with us."

I placed the penny in my pocket, and we continued to our destination. Be on the lookout for pennies from Heaven.

52

IHOP

One morning while we were in St. Louis, I decided to take the kids to IHOP for breakfast. I parked in a spot close to the front door. My son was a live wire, so I usually parked close to decrease the possibility of him running in front of a car. He was Houdini when it came to holding hands.

For some reason, I decided not to park so close, so I backed out of the spot and parked as far away as I could within the restaurant's parking lot. We settled into our seats and ordered. While enjoying our breakfast, a woman who was in the spot next to where we were originally parked pulled out and backed into a passing car. In an effort to pull back into her spot, she hunched over her steering wheel and fell unconscious. Thank goodness for alert witnesses who were able to stop her car from careening into the building and called 911. It appeared she may have had a stroke. Thank God for the warning. Listen to your hunches. Someday it may save your life and property.

53

FAMILY PETS

When my three children were young, we had two Himalayan cats, one female and one male, a domestic grey and white cat, and a male black Labrador Retriever. Occasionally at night, Amy would feel the pressure of a small dog lying on her bed. Cats are lighter on their feet. It was definitely not a large dog. The animal's weight did not seem to be more than ten pounds.

In February 2003, our twenty-one-year-old Himalayan cat, Chester, passed away. Not long afterward, I saw a translucent Chester at the foot of the stairs. When I blinked my eyes in disbelief, he was gone. All of us have felt or seen Chester on our beds. Although he was translucent, our family agreed the ghost was definitely Chester.

From time to time, our cats would look wide eyed as their eyes followed something invisible to the rest of our family. Each cat would not respond to their names being called until the object seemed to be no longer in their sight. Our dogs have been known to bark directly at something and then retreat to their beds. Animals are definitely sensitive to the spirit realm.

We adopted a Dachshund puppy soon after Chester's death. We chose a male puppy, white with brindle spots, and named him Gus. Several times during the first year, Gus noticed something near the ceiling of rooms he had access to, yet invisible to our eyes. My husband, Rachel and I were in the computer room. Gus looked at the ceiling and began to bark. The entrance and computer room shared a common wall.

He would run out of the room into the entrance and look at the ceiling. He kept barking while running back and forth from the entrance to the computer room. He saw something we could not see. After countless trips, Gus stopped due to exhaustion.

Gus lived to be seventeen-years-old. He rationalized situations like a human. In July 2019, his health noticeably began to decline. He was partially blind and deaf. He collapsed on the tiled floor. I stroked his fur and spoke softly to him. Once he regained his strength, I gave him a warm bath, telling him in so many ways how much I loved him. While holding him wrapped in a towel, I gave him last rites, making the sign of the cross on his forehead with Holy Water. Gus slept while I made an appointment with the veterinarian to arrange for him to cross the rainbow bridge.

Jack said, "Mom, give him a chance." Thank goodness I listened to my son. In a few hours, Gus bounced out of his bed energized, ready to go outside and eat. He did collapse again in October. Once again he was bathed, wrapped in a towel, and given last rites. Once again he bounced back to life. Love and prayer kept him with us for seven more months. In February 2020, he collapsed again but was unable to rally for a third time.

Amy had an Australian Shepard named Amadeus from the time he was a puppy. They loved one another. He was protective and not your average dog. Amadeus could rationalize a situation. At the age of eight, he began not to eat. His stomach appeared bloated. They took him to the veterinarian to see what was his condition. This dog breed is prone to have tumors on the kidneys. The doctor could remove them, but they would come back with a vengeance. They thought he could be treated with a prescription, but the recommendation was to put him down. It was devastating to say goodbye to a dear friend who was loved so much. When Mark and Amy returned home, their other dog, Drake joined them in their king-sized bed. Tears flowed down all their faces. Drake was so melancholy. As they lied in bed, something was forming on the bedroom ceiling. Sunlight was coming through the clear window. There was no rain or puddles outside the home. Above their bed, the image of Amadeus became clear. Thank goodness for the smart phone. The majority of its owners always seem to have a camera within reach. Mark took a few photos of their dear friend. Within the month, Drake died of a broken heart.

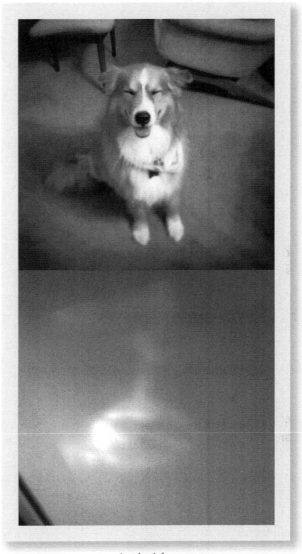

Amadeus's face

54

OGLETHORPE HOUSE

The establishment of the Savannah College of Art and Design in 1979 brought the revitalization of this colonial port city. In the 1960's, the deterioration of the downtown historic district led to an increase in crime. Drug trafficking, prostitution, and murder were prolific. The college joined forces with the city of Savannah, Georgia in the restoration of buildings spread out among the squares dotted with magnolias, southern oaks, and azaleas. SCAD's contribution brought back the beauty and prosperity of this haunted city. Ghosts from by gone eras of the historical battles, piracy, epidemics, cultural and religious diversity haunt this seemingly serene 400-year-old town. Perhaps the preservation of the buildings resulted in the disturbance of the spirit world.

My son-in-law Mark resided at the Oglethorpe House dorm during his first quarter. The building was originally a motel designed with six floors of open-air corridors lined with balconies. The motel had been a haven for crime. Student residents of Oglethorpe House have heard the sound of spectral high heeled shoes walk along the balconies. Shadow movements seen in Mark's peripheral vision would vanish when he moved for a clearer look. Students would hear a knock on their door, but no one was in sight when they opened the door to see who was there. Frequently, Mark walked through pockets of unseasonably cold air and heard the murmuring of voices in his room when he was alone.

When Mark approached the elevator, it would automatically open its doors in anticipation of his need for service. Neither he nor any other occupant had pressed the elevator button. There was no anticipated delay before the closure of its doors. When he entered, he thanked the unknown operator.

Mark had never before been afraid of heights. Living on the sixth floor brought an over-whelming fear of being close to the edge of the balcony. His fear was not rational due to the railing being four feet high. He felt drawn to the edge as if someone was coaxing him to lean just far enough to fall six floors to the parking lot. It was rumored that some residents had contacted spirits using a Ouija board. Those students who objected to this activity posted signs in the dorm asking whoever was responsible for the heightened supernatural activity to end this communication because it was affecting the other residents.

Living in a haunted dorm was not conducive for an empathic college student to study and rest, so he vacated the Oglethorpe House. If Mark ever doubted the possibility of the reality of ghosts, he left convinced of their existence.

55

THREE'S A CROWD

Mark, my daughter Amy's fiancé, lived in a nineteenth century cottage on Tatnall St. while attending the Savannah College of Art and Design in Georgia. Mark and his roommate thought a poltergeist may be attached to the house. Kitchen cabinet doors opened when Mark and his roommate knew they had closed the cabinet doors. Objects would be moved to be discovered at another location in the house. They would hear the front door shut without it opening and closing.

One Sunday evening at 11:00 P.M., Mark heard children's voices talk to Drake, Mark's boxer pup. None of the neighbors had a puppy or children. The ghost children repeatedly called, "Come here, puppy. Come here." Drake would sit wide eyed, head tilted leaning into the voices.

On another night during the spring quarter, Mark and Amy were preparing to go to bed. Mark was having a difficult time falling asleep. Images of dead bodies hanging from old oak trees appeared to him. His body felt paralyzed. He was unable to speak. Amy felt his fear and turned on the soft light on the nightstand. Out of the blue, a loud shrill cry was heard. It seemed to be nearby, outside of the house. A thick, cottage cheese textured, charcoal color vapor materialized three feet over the bed. It expanded over a period of a few minutes to be approximately four feet by one foot in size. Amy closed and opened her eyes, stunned to see the dark manifestation had not left the room.

Amy directed Mark to think only happy thoughts of their life together. Amy held Mark as they prayed to God. Together they visualized only the presence of goodness. The paralysis lifted from Mark. They were able to leave the bedroom, but the apparition followed them through a wall into the living room. Drake barked and growled at the dark cloud as it swirled close to the ceiling. Suddenly the vapor exited the house through the kitchen and then the closed back door was heard to slam shut.

I advised Amy to go to St. John the Baptist Catholic Church and get Holy Water. Place the water into a spray bottle and mist the entire house to include opening cabinet doors and drawers, under beds, in closets, and corners of the rooms. It would be helpful to also smudge the house to force the spirits to leave. The smoke from the burning white sage smudge stick would repulse the negative energy to vacate their residence.

Smudging is an ancient practice used in many cultures, including the Native Americans to ward off negative energy. Amy sprinkled and smudged every room and repeated as a mantra, "in the name of the Father, Son, and Holy Ghost, leave this house, return to your realm of existence. Leave us alone."

Mark and Amy have lived in two other homes in Savannah. Amy has practiced the smudge cleansing ritual before they moved their belongings into each new home. After this ghostly encounter, she doesn't want to take any chances.

56

LAST SUPPER

My family attended a Last Supper reenactment at the local Baptist Church in April of 2006. The backdrop was painted exactly like Michelangelo's Last Supper. The actors were costumed in the long garments of the day with hair and makeup styled to realistically depict the disciples with Christ. The audience was amazed at the ability of the actors to remain in position for so long. The only time they moved was when they spoke their lines. It was a professional performance.

I came to the play with a very constant dull ache in my lower right side of my jaw. A few weeks prior to the event, I received a dental bridge. The pain had not eased up. The dentist warned me of some discomfort for a few weeks. Thus far my prayers for pain relief went unanswered. I was regretting the bridge and thought going through life with a missing bicuspid and shifting teeth was not such a bad thing after all.

When we exited the church and began to walk to the parking lot, it occurred to me that I was no longer suffering. The constant pain that had been my unwelcome companion for the last three weeks had suddenly left me.

I believe God aided me in my recovering. Perhaps the pain would have eventually stopped, but the timing was not coincidental. I don't believe in coincidences, so I will consider it a blessing.

57

CONFIRMATION

Rachel received her confirmation as a member of the Catholic Church in May of 2008. She was sad that, unlike her older sister, there would be no grandparents to share in the celebration of this accomplishment.

After the Bishop anointed her, she walked to her assigned seat in the pew. While walking to her seat, she distinctly smelled cedar. The familiar smell brought to Rachel's mind her paternal grandparents' closets lined in cedar. The aroma always brought memories of their home. Once she returned to her seat, the image of a deceased neighbor, Mrs. O'Brien, popped into her mind. This loving neighbor was like a grandmother to Rachel. Mrs. O'Brien had given her a cross in celebration of her first communion. Rachel felt comforted knowing that she was surrounded by grandparents in Heaven who loved and supported her.

58

HURRICANE IKE EVACUATION

Houston was once again faced with another potential hurricane on Thursday, September 9th, 2008. We lived in a mandatory evacuation zone. Although my husband and I were raised in Florida, we never had been faced with fleeing our homes due to a tidal surge or hurricane force winds exceeding 130 miles per hour. This was our second evacuation in three years.

We packed two cars with our irreplaceable photos, pets, and favorite clothing. You can only pack so much. The majority of Houstonians terminated their evacuation in Dallas or San Antonio. We preferred not to stop in the hot, humid metropolitan areas. Eureka Springs, Arkansas was another six-hour drive. The beauty of the Ozark Mountains, cool summer evenings, friendly, and relaxed atmosphere was worth the extra hours on the road. Our destination was once again the Crescent Hotel.

Hurricane Ike was determined to force its way through the Midwest. Its tropical winds managed to reach us in north Arkansas. Sunday morning at 2:00 A.M., I was awoken by a repetitive drip, drip, drip sound bouncing against the wide wooden windowsill by the side of my bed. Other than the drip of water and the wind blowing against the window, the room was quiet. I looked out the window to see the garden was barely visible. The television was on when my daughter and I fell asleep, but now only the shadows of the night brought darkness to the Victorian hotel. Sometime during the night, the storm caused the power to go out.

I reached for a flashlight in order not to wake my daughter. The blowing winds had forced rain through the air conditioner vent positioned within the bottom of the window frame. I managed to make my way to the bathroom and gathered several towels to wipe up the puddle on the windowsill and unplug the air conditioner. I lied down on the bed and was shocked to see near the high Victorian ceiling glowing, whimsical-shaped hangers revolving around the room. I sat up in bed incredulous to the sight right before my eyes. I shook my head and rubbed my eyes. They were not wire, tubular plastic, or wooden hangers. They did not look real. They had curly ends on the hook and glowed. I knew I was not dreaming, especially after getting out of bed to wipe up the water.

I called to my daughter, "Rachel, Rachel, wake up! There are hangers floating around the ceiling!" It seemed several minutes elapsed to wake her from her groggy state. I was becoming more impatient fearing the apparition would disappear.

Rachel finally replied, "I don't see any hangers floating."

"How can you not see all these hangers dancing around the ceiling?" I continued to watch them teasingly teeter totter in the air. Their show was for my eyes only. Exasperated I pulled the sheets over my head and fell back to sleep.

The next evening, my son and daughter went on The Crescent Ghost Tour. My husband and I decided not to participate, since we had taken the tour twice before on previous visits. According to our children, at one point while walking the halls of The Crescent, the guide stopped outside of our room 205. The guide proceeded to speak to the tour that guests have reported seeing objects fly around the room. He continued to speak that the cleaning staff refused to work alone because of all the strange occurrences in the hotel rooms. That explained why four women cleaned in groups. I would occasionally see one woman clean one room. I thought it was unusual that it took four women to clean our room, one to unlock the door and stand by key in hand while one cleaned the bathroom and two stripped and made the beds. The fear of a ghostly encounter was their motivation to complete their tasks in record time.

On the tour of the third floor, my son, Jack, began to feel a man's hand rest upon the back of his neck, as if a father figure was walking alongside his son. The hand stayed with Paul as the group walked down the stairs to the basement. Once they reached the basement, the pressure lifted from his neck.

Our children said the guide was knowledgeable of the historical and spiritual background of the hotel. There were no orbs visible with the naked eye or drained batteries of digital cameras nor the smell of tobacco wafting through the halls. Smoking was no longer permitted within the rooms, but that never stopped the ghosts from smoking on previous tours. The confirmation that others have experienced objects float in the room was reassuring. Every trip to The Crescent Hotel has given our family gifts of different sights, sounds, and smells. The spirits seem to be cognizant that we share our plane with the dead, and they in turn enjoy relating to the living, watching our reaction to their spectral activity.

59

HURRICANE IKE REPAIRS

Our community in Houston, Texas was severely affected by Hurricane Ike. We could not return to Houston for almost a week. The area was declared uninhabitable. There was no electricity or water. The majority of the streets were blocked by barricades. The remaining two streets entering our neighborhood were guarded by the Texas Highway Patrol who questioned all vehicle occupants, regarding their identification as residents.

We could see the water through the framework of other homes, one street south of our house. Several sections of our wooden fence had fallen, in addition a few roof shingles were blown away. It was the third week of September. The heat and humidity plus the buzz of mosquitoes made life unbearable. Our generator ran several fans that helped to relieve us from the summer heat. My husband and children worked hours outside to remove the broken fence posts and concrete from the thick gumbo clay. The installation of fence panels and new slats had replaced the nakedness of our back yard by the second weekend of our return. Everyone was weary of the hard work required to return our yards to their pre-hurricane condition.

Paul used his father's hammer to repair the wooden fence. The hammer must have been at least fifty-five-years-old. Although his father was a U.S. Post Office employee, he also had a side job as a carpenter to supplement his income to provide for his family of seven.

When one typically works at a desk in the comfort of air conditioning, manual labor takes its toll on the body. My husband prepared to sleep that night with a sock rolled into a ball held in each hand to prevent his hands from clenching into fists. Exhausted physically and emotionally, Paul fell into a deep sleep.

The next morning, he said to me, "I dreamed of my father last night."

Paul spoke of standing alongside his father in the front yard of his boyhood home. The house appeared as it did in the 1960's, light green asbestos shingles with white trim. Paul looked in his early fifties as he did at the time of the hurricane. His father also appeared as he did when he was in his early fifties. Father and son, side by side, each of a different time, yet equal in age and life experience.

Nathan said, "I am proud of the man you have become. You have done what is necessary to provide for your family." They did not touch, but the love and understanding between the two men gave Paul such comfort. He was thankful for his father's blessing.

60

LILY DALE

During the summer of 2015, I visited my daughter and son-in law in Pennsylvania. We often took excursions as part of my visits. Niagara Falls was on my bucket list.

As the sun would shine upon the falls, rainbows appeared within the mist. Riding on the Maid of the Mist, a boat to carry tourists, we would see the breathtaking views of the falls, a heavenly experience not to be forgotten.

While headed back to their home, we stopped by another bucket list destination, Lily Dale, New York. This Victorian Spiritualist town of close to 300 residents is on Lake Cassadaga. Many psychics live in Lily Dale during the summer and Cassadaga, Florida during the winter.

Open during the warmer months, guest psychics come to speak, heal, and hold workshops at Lily Dale. There are restaurants, gift shops, and a hotel. An event was planned at the Forest Temple venue. Mediums give messages as those in attendance sit on wooden benches outside under the trees. Although it was the middle of summer, a gentle cool breeze kept us free from the otherwise sweltering temperatures.

Not everyone in attendance receives a message. This can be disappointing, but oh so rewarding if you are a recipient. My adult children and I sat listening to the mediums perform their gifts. Soon after we arrived, the medium pointed to us that she had a message to deliver.

"There is a man here, a fatherly figure, who had lung and heart problems. Does this sound familiar?" Once validating her question, she continued. "Have you just visited Niagara Falls?" I nodded in the affirmative. "He joined your family to share in this experience." Once again I received a gift that confirmed even after death our deceased loved ones watch over us.

61

SHOPPING

My daughter, Rachel, attended college in Florida. We enjoyed shopping on Saturdays at an outdoor market along the St. Johns River. Shopping under a bridge added to the comfort. There were crafts, art work, jewelry, produce, and products galore.

Rachel and I strolled down the walkways until we saw two women sitting at empty card tables. One woman called to me, "You have someone from the spirit world walking with you."

"What is he wearing?"

"Khaki pants and a plaid shirt."

That was all I needed to hear that once again my dad was hanging out with us. Khaki pants and a plaid shirt were his uniform. It gives me comfort knowing Dad enjoys tagging along.

62

HENNY PENNY

While preparing dinner one late afternoon in 2012, my son Jack and I heard the very loud sound of a horn. We went out the back door to see where it was coming from. It wasn't a melody playing, just the sound of a horn coming from all directions and not from a distance. No one was in the backyard. We only lived two blocks from Johnson Space Center. Could the noise be coming from a normally very quiet government facility?

The sky was clear, not even a bird could be seen or heard. Maybe my imagination was beginning to get the best of me, but it sounded similar to the Hebrew horn called the shofar. Was this the sound of the ram's horn announcing a preeminent battle? The image of the four horsemen of the apocalypse came to mind. I don't normally jump to biblical conclusions. I don't know for how long it continued. There was nothing I could do about it, so we went inside the house, and I continued to cook dinner. Eventually it stopped. None of my Christian friends said a word about the sound, but I had not asked them for fear of being laughed at. A few years later, while researching this phenomenon, I discovered other people from all over the world shared similar experiences but during different seasons and years. Could this be the beginning of the end? Time will tell.

63

HOMECOMING

Do you remember in Chapter 4 my account of the woman in 19th century clothing lecturing a few boys? In the years that followed, I received a subscription to Colonial Home magazine in the 1980s. There was no way I could validate my past life family's existence, until flipping through the pages, a home caught my eye. Deep in my soul, I knew this house. The architecture is Greek Revival, four stately Corinthian columns spanned the front, and the stone is painted a golden yellowish color. I don't believe it was that color in the early 1800's. An expansive lawn gradually sloped down towards a road that ran parallel to a body of water later confirmed to be the Ohio River.

The mighty Ohio River made me feel so sad. I wasn't sure why I felt so depressed. The feeling lingered for a while. We did not have a personal computer at this time. I knew nothing about the location and history of Madison, Indiana. The town was now on my bucket list.

After visiting relatives in Pennsylvania in July of 2017, Paul, Jack and I set out to visit Madison, Indiana. If you appreciate small historic towns, this is a must see. We dropped off our luggage at the Hillside Inn before we set out to explore the town and have dinner.

The next morning, my husband and I began early to make the most of our day. I was almost giddy by the time we arrived at the mansion. It felt as if I was coming home. First and foremost was the staircase. My memory went back to the day I was standing on the stairs, where I reprimanded the boys. In that life, I was also petite, so I stood on the first or second steps to tower over the boys. For most of the tour, we were the only visitors. What a great opportunity to absorb the memory of this stately house. In the dining room, across from the staircase was a painting of my past life son, John, whom the tour guide mentioned tragically drowned in the Ohio River. Now I had confirmation of the sadness I felt when thoughts of the rushing river brought to mind the loss of a son. My belief is the boys had a temptation to play by the river. This was a continual source of worry for me. Perhaps the funeral attendance in the regression was related to the deep grief I felt for the loss of my son.

As we walked outside, I looked to the left at the bottom of the stairs where in a dream I once wore a long white dress and sat on a blanket with my husband and children. The young, handsome, dark-haired man in my dream written in Chapter 44 was the same man, James Lanier, whose wife was named Elizabeth. The sweet memory of my past life family laughing while enjoying the view of riverboats paddling down the strong current felt so familiar of my time living in Madison.

During the regression, I had felt Elizabeth experienced respiratory problems. The visit confirmed Elizabeth died from tuberculosis at the age of forty-eight, ten years after John drowned.

The cemetery was the next stop on my sentimental tour. Springdale Cemetery is the oldest and closest to the historic town district. Paul drove the car slowly along the cemetery lane. When we reached the center, I decided to get out of the car and pivot until I felt drawn to the Lanier gravesites. It was as if I was guided to an area elevated with stone sides surrounding the family plots. The familiarity was comforting as I walked across the cemetery. This may sound unbelievable, but this is the sensation I experienced as I began to get closer to the gravesites. Once I stepped up onto the raised burial site, I walked directly to the opposite side and found the etched tombstone of John James Lanier, drowned at the age of seven, on April 20th, 1836. His gravestone was confirmation of my memory of a dark day that never left my soul. Close by laid the tombstone of Elizabeth Lanier, deceased April 15th, 1846, almost ten years to the day her son had drowned. The confirmation of John's and Elizabeth's lives and untimely deaths filled me with sorrow yet relief.

At the mansion gift shop, Paul and I bought a book written by James Lanier. James was in a train accident, but he was not injured. He was definitely a businessman who served the state as a banker, lawyer, ownership of a pork packing company, and involved with railroad development in Indiana. To my knowledge in this life, I am not related to the Lanier family. My pioneer ancestors came to Indiana in the 1840s. My mother was born in Indiana, and my parents were married in Clark County adjacent to Jefferson County, Indiana where Madison is located. This is the only connection I am aware of as the truth. Over fifty years ago, my journey first began with dreams of a life in a stately home, which led to a magazine article, regression, and travel to Madison, Indiana.

Lanier Mansion, Madison, Indiana

Staircase in the Lanier Mansion

Springdale Cemetery, Madison, Indiana

167

Gravesite of Elizabeth Lanier

64

OUR FATHER

In October of 2018, I fell asleep on the couch watching ghost shows. I didn't know what time it was, but I woke up with a jolt, then found myself paralyzed. All I could move were my eyes. What I saw is beyond my imagination, a black hooded cloak with a skull and skeletal body suspended two feet above me. No wonder I was frozen. My thoughts immediately turned to prayer. With my eyes shut, I silently thought the words to "Our Father," the cloaked skeleton vanished. My body was free to move.

The first words out of my mouth were, "What did I just see?" It had been at least thirty years since I had dreamed of the Devil's face up close taunting me. I no longer watch scary TV shows before bed. Earlier in the evening, my destination is my bedroom. A spray bottle of Holy Water now sets on my dresser. Periodically our bedrooms are anointed with Holy Water, thus far no more nightmarish visitations.

65

BE ALERT

My brother-in-law, Thomas, passed away in March 2019. Our family was traveling to attend the funeral service. We were headed west on the highway, then stopped at a traffic light. The road rarely has a high volume of traffic but does have a lengthy wait time at the lights.

Preoccupied with his thoughts of the funeral, my husband proceeded forward as a car on the eastbound lane began to turn north. As the white sedan began a left-hand turn, its horn blew. My husband yelled, "I've run the red light." In turn he blew our car's horn to sound the alarm, knowing he had made a mistake.

As I looked over at the approaching car, my view was of the car's left front tire well a few feet from our driver's door. A collision was inevitable.

Within a split second, we found ourselves translated a block away. I turned my head and could still see the white sedan completing its turn. I've heard of others being transported to avoid an accident. We were grateful that God was watching over us.

66
RETURN TO TEXAS

A few years ago, we returned to Texas to attend a wedding of one of Jack's childhood friends. The next day, we went to south Texas to check on a tombstone for my great-grandmother. Several of the cousins had met on a genealogy website. For some reason, my great-grandmother did not have a tombstone, so we pulled together our funds and ordered a lovely one to honor our ancestor. There was a mystery surrounding her death. She had been gravely ill. Eventually our great-grandfather admitted her to a hospital in Galveston where she died in 1901.

I located my ancestor's home in a rural community. How pleased I was to see a Texas historical marker beside the entrance. The owner answered my knock on the front door and smiled as I introduced myself as the great-granddaughter of the John and Cherry Horton indicated on the Texas plaque. She invited me in and showed me the original master bedroom, kitchen, and living area of this pioneer home. I imagined my deceased relatives gathered at the table eating a hearty Texan breakfast before they began their chores tending to their horse ranch and red grapefruit groves.

The owner must have felt comfortable with me after we spoke for a while. She began to tell me a story of whom she believed to be Cherry. The owner was convalescing on the sofa. She saw a translucent woman with light hair wearing a long white night gown leave the bedroom, cross the living room into the kitchen, where she disappeared. I believed her story.

Since she was resting on the sofa due to her health, perhaps this triggered the spirit of Cherry to show herself.

I thanked the sweet lady for allowing me to see my ancestors' home. The trip satisfied my love of genealogy and supernatural experiences.

John & Cherry Horton with children in the 1880s

Horton Homestead today

67

THINNING OF THE VEIL

One afternoon in the summer of 2019, I was upstairs in the master bedroom folding laundry and tidying up. No one else was in the house. My husband and daughter were at work while my son was outside enjoying the pool. I clearly heard my name spoken from the hallway. A masculine voice similar to my father's called, "Jane." This took me by surprise.

I walked into the hall and said, "Hello. Is that you, Dad?" There was no reply. I returned to the bedroom with the anticipation to hear another call from across the veil.

That same week, I was on my Meals on Wheels route. My last customer was an amazing WW II veteran. Our chats were the highlight of my day. He opened up to me that he had been in his study working on his computer. He heard the voice of his deceased wife call out his name. Her voice was clear and distinct as it came from the bedroom; she passed a few years prior. I shared my encounter with the voice of my dad calling my name.

Why had we both experienced a love one call out our names within the same week? Had the veil thinned to permit clairaudient contact?

68

TRAFFIC LIGHT

One day in February of 2019, I was running errands. There was hardly a cloud in sight. The stoplight turned red, so I was prepared to wait a few minutes. While gazing at the sky above the traffic light, a vaporous image appeared in the distance. The formation began to take on the shape of a brownish golden structure resembling a stone arch.

As I looked through the arch, another shape began to appear. The vision quickly took the appearance of a golden cross gliding up to the arch. I was focusing on this heavenly sight, not wanting to proceed through the green light. Once my eyes looked to the road and then returned up to the sky, the image had disappeared. I was thankful that God took the time to reach out to me for this brief encounter.

CONCLUSION

After you have read my family's experiences with the supernatural, I hope you may be more receptive to your own encounters. You are not alone. You can accept these experiences as being supernatural. They are real, but the source does not come from our plane of existence. We will not entirely grasp this concept until it is our time to cross over to the spirit realm.

On the other hand, you may be thinking that I am off my rocker. It is your choice to think what you want. Seeing for yourself is 100 percent of believing what you see. I have attempted to demonstrate I am a sane individual. I started writing this book for my family and not for the public to judge.

I ask God each day to guide me. He has the power. He loves us. We must show him our love and faith. He will lead us on the right path. It is a good thing to be faced with some struggle. We can't expect to be happy every day of our lives. Happiness is fleeting. Sometimes heart ache and pain strengthen our will to carry on. There are lessons we all must learn: patience, forgiveness, love, and faith in what we cannot see. Reincarnation allows the spirit to return in an attempt to achieve these lessons. The experiences are natural, but can be amplified through the supernatural.

Religion that is found in traditional churches does not readily enable us to experience a one-on-one personal experience with God. Attending church does play an important role in building our knowledge of the historical and inspirational significance of Christianity. If you receive a supernatural experience in church that is the icing on the cake.

Supernatural activity can be experienced anywhere as long as one has an open sincere heart. God does work miracles in today's world. Don't explain a blessing from God as being a coincidence. You must have faith in God. Please be open to Him. Believe your children when they speak to you of their thoughts and experiences. My children have never given me a reason to doubt their sincerity. I advise my children to listen to their inner voice.

Sometimes God speaks to us through telepathy, but other times His voice can be heard out loud only to those who are meant to hear Him. If you have self-doubts, keep in mind the memories of experiences that stay with you validate the authenticity of the experience.

I can't conjure up a dream or on demand read someone's past, present, or future from tea leaves, palmistry, or tarot cards. It doesn't work like that for me. It just happens when I least expect it. We all have the ability to develop our psychic talents. The question is do we want to? It is a big responsibility. If God wants me to be aware of perils or life altering events that might befall someone in our family, I have faith that He will let me know or give me the strength to handle the situation.

I have never allowed a Ouija board in my home or approved of séances. I have never set up a tape recorder in Rachel's room. I do not want to introduce or encourage communication with potential negative spirits. Although we have experienced more than most people admit to, I do not want to encourage it in my home. I don't want to open a portal to a troubled spirit or something who has never lived as a person that may prove to be a negative force. I believe the spirits who do visit our home are not threatening. I believe they watch over us. If there is tension, depression, or arguments in your home, consider smudging to cleanse and eradicate the negativity.

I have told all my children that if they are ever at a party and someone wants to crank up the party a notch by introducing these dangerous games, they should say that they need to call home to be picked up. Amy and Rachel have done just that. Their peers respected them. It made them think of the possible repercussions. I have explained these are not games but tools used to communicate with the dead. It may not bring back Aunt Cleo. A demonic entity or evil spirit may use this as a ruse to cause havoc. If one is compelled out of curiosity to participate in this activity, please do it in a neutral environment with an experienced medium. Never, never allow children to be in close proximity. This may not prevent the entities from attaching to you. A spirit may ride piggy back into your homes. To prevent this, an experienced medium will begin each meditation or reading session with a prayer and ask that you be surrounded with white light and be free of all negativity. Ask God to connect you with your guardian angel.

It is inevitable my family will continue to experience the supernatural. Future experiences will hopefully be written and passed down to the next generation. It is my wish as my family tree continues to branch, my descendants will learn from their supernatural genealogical history and always walk in the path of God protected by the white light.